Emerging Proud Press
The Enterprise Centre
Norwich NR4 7TJ
United Kingdom

ISBN: 978-1-9160860-8-1 (paperbook)
ISBN: 978-1-9160860-9-8 (ebook)

www.EmergingProud.com

KindaPROUD
Stories of Hope & Transformation

DEDICATION

This book is dedicated to people worldwide who have experienced any level of sight loss, but specifically to help inspire and encourage visually impaired young people to strive for your goals and achieve your dreams. Through these stories of people from an array of backgrounds, different countries, with different sight disorders either from birth, degenerative over time, or through a sudden accident, we hope that any young person with sight loss will believe that NOTHING IS IMPOSSIBLE.

We also hope that our "inspiration warriors" will encourage sighted people to go for their goals, and not allow anything to hold you back. If we can do what we have done in the face of adversity, we believe you can achieve anything too. Time can always be made, and money does not make the world go round - passion does.

"The best and most beautiful things in the world cannot be seen or even touched - they must be felt with the heart"

— Helen Keller

This series of books is dedicated to maintaining the integrity of the voices of the people that have shared their stories. The stories shared are real life situations and some of them may contain language that could be triggering for some people, such as suicidal behaviour, and other upsetting content. We recognise that each individual taking part in and reading this book will be at different stages of their transformation journey, and we want to honour that where we're all at is perfectly okay. If you want some extra advice or support links, please seek support from the 'Resources' section in the back of the book.

Praise for this KindaProud Pocket Book

"We 100% believe that we are stronger when navigating blindness together. This little book channels the strength of many and will improve and expand the quality of life for all who read it. Thank you for bringing together a diverse group sharing a common theme of thriving with sight loss."

Kim Owens from www.NavigatingBlindness.com

"Each unique story included within this book demonstrates resilience and the ability to overcome obstacles at the highest level. We know that the power of sport can change lives for the better but that the powers of self-belief and courage of conviction can help change the world."

Alaina MacGregor, CEO of British Blind Sport

"I think this book is well needed as someone who has sight loss it's great to know you're not alone and there are many others like you out there. The eye inspire book shows that anything is possible with sight loss and that we still have vision even if we don't have sight"

Daniel Williams – Visualise Training & Consultancy

Contents

About our Emerging Proud Book Series

Why do we need 'Pocket Books of Hope and Transformation'? There is a rising epidemic of mental health problems in our society, and alongside it a pervasive negative prognosis message that goes out to those who are struggling emotionally. It's our shared belief, due to our personal experiences, that one of the most important elements of getting back on a road to recovery (and ultimately transformation) is to hear personal stories of HOPE from those who have been there before and not just survived, but thrived.

Each Pocket Book has its own Rep; a Peer who has personal experience of 'coming through' the theme of that specific book. These are the 6 books in the series, currently published or in the process of being published:-

- #Emerging Proud through NOTEs (Non-Ordinary Transcendent Experiences)

- #Emerging Proud through Disordered Eating, Poor Body Image and Low Self- Esteem

- #Emerging Proud through Suicide

- #Emerging Proud through Trauma and Abuse

- #Emerging Proud through Eye Sight Loss

- Muslims #Emerging Proud through Mental Distress

What are the main Aims and Objectives of this Pocket Book series?

To relieve people of the distress associated with transformational crises by offering authentic examples of personal stories and resources to engender hope and initiate recovery.

To decrease stigma, improve wellbeing and influence the saving of lives by providing a more compassionate and positive conceptual framework for emotional distress.

To use the profits from book sales to continue to distribute free books, and hence messages of HOPE, to support organisations, and those in need, all around the world.

All of the stories in this book have been kindly donated by peers who have personally experienced this specific theme of sight loss and 'emerged transformed'; dedicated to giving hope that there is light at the end of the tunnel to others who may still be struggling. This book series was seed-funded by *The Missing Kind* charity.

Meet the Project's Founder

My name is Katie Mottram and I'm the Founder of the #Emerging Proud campaign, through which the KindaProud book series has been birthed. #Emerging Proud is a grassroots social movement aimed at: 'Re-framing mental distress as a catalyst for positive transformation'; providing a platform for people who have 'emerged transformed' through a personal crisis and feel called to share their story and give hope to others.

I was called to start this movement due to finding that re-framing my own crisis as a transformational growth process (which still continues!), and hearing the experiences of others, was the thing that helped me to connect with my authentic Self, and start to live the life I was born to live.

When I experienced a personal crisis in 2008, what I needed was a message of HOPE, that all would be okay, not that there was anything 'wrong' with me. I needed to connect with others who had been through similar challenges and were able to walk alongside me whilst I found my own way out of the darkness.

In the last decade, it has been through my own research; looking at more empowering ways of understanding what happened to me, my reactions to it, and how to go about self-healing, in addition to connecting with my amazing peers and listening to their stories, that has really set me on my own path of transformation. This feels like the complete opposite of what I had been told was helpful whilst working within mental health services for 15 years previously. Hence my passion to provide others with the tools that helped me not only to survive, but to thrive and love life.

You can read my full story in my own book, *Mend the Gap: A transformative journey from deep despair to spiritual awakening*, which I published in 2014.

I truly hope that this book, and the others in the 'Pocket Books of Hope and Transformation' series, inspires and supports you in your own evolutionary journey…

And, remember: let that light you hold deep inside shine unapologetically bright - we were ALL born to shine our light in the world - in whatever way that feels right to you!

Find out more about the campaign and what we're up to at: **www.emergingproud.com**

Meet our Peer Pocket Book Rep, Yvette Chivers from Cambridge, UK

When the going gets tough, the tough certainly get going! That perfectly describes our incredible Rep for this inspirational book, Yvette ...

All Contributors in this book, in addition to our Rep Yvette, have faced going blind at some point in their lives, and all the turmoil that foreboding brings. But rather than become victims to futures of darkness, each and every one of them have used this darkness to spark their inner light.

For Yvette, this inner light set her on a creative path of utilising another of her senses to another level. Here she sings her personal song...

I was born with quite severe myopia (short-sight) and a lazy right eye, so eye clinic hospital visits became the norm as I went through the toddler-phase and into nursery. Through junior school I vehemently refused to wear my national-health, thick-rimmed, thick-lensed spectacles and absolutely hated the patch I had to wear regularly to ease the lazy eye that continued to make me squint. In the 1980s, being the 'speccy' one at school was a feat to deal with in itself!

When I turned 16, and contact-lenses became available to me, it was like a new lease of life. I felt more confident, and less of a nerd. I felt like I had transformed into a different person. The negative connotations I had developed about glasses and generally having bad eyesight had stuck with me, but at last now I could shake that off. Little did I know that I had a LOT more to contend with in the future with regards to my sight and my self-belief.

I was diagnosed with Retinitis Pigmentosa (RP) after a routine eye test at a high street opticians whilst I was living and working in London, having moved there from Cambridge to start my career in creative advertising. The optician spotted something in the back of my eye and referred me to Moorfields Eye Hospital for further examination. From when I became a teenager, I had seen tiny white flashing lights in my vision: the only way to describe it is like a static TV screen – the information is there, but with millions of minuscule gaps in it. But

I had always put it down to being part of being short sighted, and I noticed it more when I was tired.

Unfortunately, I experienced a difficult diagnosis period - Moorfields sent the results to a consultant at a private hospital I was then with, who said there was nothing wrong with me. But by this point I wanted a second opinion, and my childhood optician back in Cambridge confirmed it as textbook RP.

The following month I was made redundant from my dream job. A few months passed in a daze and I moved back to my family home, as I was just treading water in London and spiralling out of control mentally. After going back to the hospital eye clinic that I attended so regularly as a child, for confirmation of the degenerative disorder and to gain some form of support, I was told that generally, with RP, most sight would be lost within 10 years' time. I was just 24 and thought my life was over, or at least thought that the life I wanted to have was gone.

A lot of the rest of my 20s are still a blur, but during this time I developed a love and skill for DJing. I think it was the one thing I could rely on, knowing that I still had my hearing. I had always been a music lover, collecting vinyl as a teenager and taking my second-hand Philips flat-pack record player from University to every shared house I lived in. My love of Motown and old soul records was evidently passed down from my dad, and back in Cambridge I started event nights playing out Motown, funk and soul with other DJs who were into the same music. I was also a keen club-goer and my DJing soon developed into playing dance music. I really have no idea how, but through my passion and perseverance, I ended up running my own monthly club night in Cambridge for ten years, and DJing in super-clubs such as the Ministry of Sound in London, warehouse parties in Berlin and on amazing stages at huge festivals including the Secret Garden Party.

I do believe that this absolute love of the music, and my no-fear attitude, enabled me to go into situations not really knowing if I could achieve the goal at hand, but just giving it a damn good go anyway. When you are presented with losing your sight, you can either let it consume you, or you can just take every opportunity possible. I did a trek in the Himalayas and The Andes for charity; I did crazy things like bungee jumps, skydiving and wing-walking. I wanted to experience as much as I possibly could before my sight totally left me.

Don't get me wrong, it took me a long time to get to that "no fear" point. I was depressed for a long time, I couldn't or wouldn't get into any meaningful relationships because I didn't believe anyone would want to be with a girl who would be blind soon. I had huge issues with my self-esteem and unfortunately self-medicated on binge drinking and other forms of escapism. Apparently, a lot of degenerative eye-sight disorders come with a denial phase, and I remember being told that RP denial is roughly 10 years. I am not kidding when I say that the veil of total uncertainty finally lifted when I was in my early thirties, almost exactly ten years after I was initially diagnosed.

From this point, and leading up to founding the project Eye Inspire, I realised that without the support I had from friends and family, as well as meeting other young people with sight-loss, and from counselling from charities such as Cam Sight in Cambridge, I would not have regained the confidence that I am so glad I now have. I managed to set up and run an international music remix project that is now in its 10th year, working with amazing famous music artists and producers. I work with music colleges, amazing electronic music labels and large professional music equipment brands on various creative projects and events. I went to Japan on a four-day round trip as the agent of an internationally renowned electronic artist, which was a crazy experience. I feel extremely lucky to be in this position of working in an industry that I love so much, and over time I have created my own role which enables me to work within my own abilities and mobility – I now have a guide dog, who does come with me to many events and music talks that I deliver, but I definitely don't take him clubbing!

I wanted to give back in some way, and to encourage other young people with sight-loss that anything really is possible. There will be sad and difficult experiences, but whatever you want to do, you can achieve. There is no boundary to your capabilities. Most sighted people haven't been to the places I have been or achieved what I have in terms of music or career, and it's truly been down to a bit of hard work, a sprinkling of luck, but fundamentally a lot of passion. I have never had much money, I've not been in a privileged position that way, but I have still gone to Peru and Goa on my own when I simply and firmly got the idea in my head. Where there is a will, there is a way. And from my story, and the many amazing stories in this book from people I have met on my own journey, I hope that you will be inspired to go for your dreams and aspirations. If you want it, you will most definitely achieve it. I am a great believer in a positive mental attitude.

Please do contact us via the website below if you are a visually impaired young person who would like any help in training or work experience in an area you are passionate about. We want to support any young person with sight loss to gain the links and contacts to help achieve their goals. We will be planning a series of talks to youth groups in the UK and internationally, for young people with sight loss, and some talk-based events in the UK which will be live-streamed on social media for global viewing and listening, featuring some of our amazing contributors from this book. For information about these events, do visit www.eyeinspire.org and to join the newsletter. If indeed you are reading (or listening to) this book after the events have taken place, the recorded videos and audio will be available on the website.

Yvette Chivers, AKA DJ MissChivers xx

www.eyeinspire.org

Follow Yvette's DJ career and Eye Inspire's insp-eye-ring work at:

Facebook: www.facebook.com/djmisschivers and

www.facebook.com/eyeinspire2020

Twitter: @misschiversuk and @eyeinspire2020

Instagram: @misschiversuk and @eyeinspire2020

MissChivers logo, a high-heeled boot with headphones on the top.

I hope you enjoy the many stories of inspiration in this book, and I'll finish my contribution with one of my favourite quotes:

"Sometimes you need to shake up your own world and the people around you"

– Sander Kleinenburg

Justin Bishop from Las Vegas, USA, felt the fear and did it anyway, and now he uses his intuition to keep his dream alive

Justin knows how it feels to lose everything you've worked hard for, and discover that this does not have to mean the end; in fact, it can be the beginning of amazing opportunities. Being told he'd go blind when he was a child led Justin to push himself hard to be the best he could be before sight loss took hold. After a journey through depression, feelings of failure and dreams lost, Justin's determination has led him back to his original destination. Justin's inspiring story proves that anything is possible if you follow your dreams...

Imagine sitting in a doctor's office being told you have a genetic disease that causes blindness. Now imagine being eight years old and being told you will be blind one day. It is pretty hard as an eight year old to think about adulthood and the consequences of a genetic disease. They might as well have told a kid they would also have a mortgage and must pay taxes. Well, that is what happened to me. Twenty-five years ago I was told I had Retinitis Pigmentosa and it would change my life forever. As a child I was ignorant of what that would mean for me. That ignorance would turn into denial. That denial eventually turned into acceptance, then depression, and then back to a realization that I could have a normal life. My name is Justin Bishop, and today I am a blind amateur skateboarder.

When I was diagnosed with RP it really meant nothing to me. I understood it was important, and it was always in the back of my head, but just did not affect me. This ignorance allowed me to have a pretty normal childhood. In my pre-teens I found my passion for skateboarding and it consumed my life from that point on.

The first time RP started to affect me was years later when I was seventeen and driving home from work late one night. I realized I could not see very well in the dark anymore. My drive home was stressful, terrifying, and downright dangerous. One of the first things RP effects, is night blindness, which is your ability to have your eyes adjust in the dark. Up until this point, I had been ignorant of my condition. I carried on with my denial and spent another year driving home in the dark, when I should not have. All because, I was not ready to admit I was becoming visually impaired.

When I was eighteen, I admitted to myself, my family, and my work that I could not drive at night anymore. I realized one day soon I would be blind. Those words I heard ten years ago were coming true. I will be blind. I knew I was in a race for time, so I doubled down on skateboarding and what I loved so I could have as much of it whilst I could see.

Around this time in my life, I was a mad man when it came to skateboarding. This sport consumed my every waking hour. If I wasn't working, I was on my board. I picked up some local sponsors, won some competitions, and made my dad proud. Fulfilling my dream of being a skateboarder before I lost my sight was really important to me.

When I was twenty, another major loss happened to my sight. I lost my driver's license because a milky gloss started to happen to my eyes, and I was no longer able to pass the DMV eye exam. Everything I was looking at started to look as if I was looking through a dirty window. It was blurry, and nothing was defined. Even though I lost my license, I could still see enough to skateboard. Not being able to drive, and now not being able to work, I went harder on my skateboarding. At this point, I was spending every hour skateboarding -

I was good at it too. That is, until I was twenty-five. I remember this week vividly, because it was such a dramatic loss in such a short time. Usually with RP, it is a short loss over a long period of time. You don't notice what you can't see until your next eye exam or test. In one week I lost most of my sight, independence, and what felt like most of my life.

It was a summer day in Las Vegas. Nice and hot at the skatepark. I was there just skating, and practicing, and I realized my skateboard was getting blurrier. I couldn't really tell where the top of the board was when I flipped it. I remember telling myself to shake it off and get some sleep. The next day I was there, and I realized I couldn't see the ramp or rails directly in front of me. I could only see them out of the corner of my eyes. My board was gone, the park was disappearing, and it hit me. My skating days were over. Everything I worked fifteen years to gain was all gone in a matter of 48 hours. I was too blind to see what I was doing.

With an eye exam, I found out I no longer had central vision. The RP started to fully affect my central sight. I could only see out of the corner of my eyes. It hit me all at once. This has happened, I am blind now. I wish at this point I could tell you I was strong, picked myself right back up, and learned how to be blind, but that is not true. When a human loses anything they grieve, and I went into a depression.

I had no confidence during this depression. I stayed this way for months, until my dad sat down and talked to me man to man. He told me something very important. He said that it was ok to be sad. What happened was a big deal. But I had been sad long enough. I needed to realize I was not the first person to go blind. That statement woke me up. It made me realize life was not over and I had to keep going. The next day I did everything in my power to start learning how to be blind. From getting my first cane, to taking mobility training, and learning how to make technology more accessible. Most importantly I learned how to live an independent lifestyle. This process did not happen overnight, but after two years I was a confident blind individual.

Although I retained my confidence and some independence, I still struggled with being fulfilled. I wanted to contribute and get a job. Trying to obtain a job for someone blind or visually impaired is one of the hardest obstacles I have encountered. Either you are overqualified for tasks they would trust a blind person with, or you are flatly denied an opportunity of trying a position just because you are holding a white cane. After months of being denied work, even washing dishes at a bar, I finally had my luck turn around. I came across a job opening for an ABA therapist in the autism community. They were looking for someone to teach kids on the spectrum how to skateboard - a skill I had spent much of my life honing. Obviously, this seemed like a dream job for me with my background. I applied and was fortunate to get an interview. I wish more blind people could have interviewed with the owner I have had the privilege to work for. He was understanding and, instead of turning me away, he gave me an opportunity to prove I could do the job. A chance to show that my sight did not stop me from teaching. I was doing my dream job teaching children how to skateboard, at an amazing company that supported me by making what I needed accessible. I had joined a community that fully accepted me.

Even though I was working around skateboarding, I still did not get back on the board myself. Emotionally I was too hurt about how much I had lost when I lost my sight. That all changed when one day at work a friend asked me if I could still drop in on a halfpipe. I told him, no, probably not: if I can't see the ground, I can't see where I am going. I knew skateboarding was over for me. As he also had a passion for skateboarding, he would not accept no for an answer, no matter how many times I said it. So, I tried to drop in. I remember grabbing the skateboard, setting the tail on the coping to drop in, and standing up on top of the board ready to drop in with so much fear. Not fear that I would get hurt, but the fear of looking stupid in front of everyone. I shook it off and went for it. I dropped in for the first time in years, and I landed it. A flood of ecstasy hit me at the same time I realized the other side of the halfpipe was coming up. So, I quickly prepared to do a rock and roll on the other side of the coping. When I got there, I got into the rock and roll, but I got hung up and fell straight to the bottom of the halfpipe. Everyone rushed to me to make sure I was ok, just to find me with tears streaking my cheeks and a huge smile on my face. Laughing and crying at the realization of how much I loved skateboarding. I love the successes, and even the failures of getting hurt. I was laughing because I was so happy I had found my love of skateboarding again and crying because I was so angry for ever having let it go. So angry that my biggest fear was looking stupid in front of other people. From that day on, I was like a sixteen year old kid again, skateboarding every day. Re-learning tricks I had already mastered, now having to use timing and pure luck. This is the part of my life that I realized how lucky I am. Most people only get to learn how to skateboard once, and I got to learn twice. With all the same joy and excitement I had as a young boy.

From this point on I started skating with my friends again. Getting out of the house and making skate videos and reconnecting with the skate community. Before I knew it, I had companies reaching out wanting to sponsor me. A friend did an article about my skating, and that sparked an interest from Zappos, Electric sunglasses, Nixon, Element Skateboards, Nike SB, Independent Trucks, and many more. Now I am an Amateur Skateboarder getting to travel the world doing what I love. If I can pass one thing on from my story it is to just keep moving forward. You never know what possibility you might be missing due to your fear holding you back.

Follow Justin on social media here:

Facebook: www.facebook.com/justinvegaslights
Instagram: @justinthebishop
Twitter: @justinthebishop

Lachi from New York, USA, is more than proud of sharing her story to inspire you to believe in your dreams

Lachi hasn't allowed the stigma imposed on her at a young age to prevent her from pursuing and achieving her dream of becoming a successful musician and author, and she takes pride in encouraging YOU to do the same...

At eight I dreamed of being a musician with a fancy management team and my own recording studio, being a published author with my own agent, and traveling the world for my art. But it was also at eight that I realized few of my favorite singers or writers were female, fewer were black, and absolutely none were blind. When I turned on the television and saw all the perfect people, I thought to myself, "That could never be me."

Early Days

I was born with a rare eye disease called coloboma, which left me legally blind. I could see up to about as far as my outstretched hand. This made it hard to read at pace with other kids. And the need for extra devices, coupled with the frequent visits from social workers, made it tough not to be different. Like many with disabilities, while my visual impairment made it difficult to see, my real trouble growing up was social. That is the overarching backdrop of my story.

Was I bullied? Yes, early and often. I have a lazy eye, much lazier back then. Or rather, it was the opposite of lazy, as it actively did its own thing. Because of this, I was given the ugly kid treatment or the slow kid treatment, depending. Which was tough for a girl that had all the pretty girl traits, just no idea how to manifest them. Or a girl who had all the smarty-pants fixings, just no idea how to outwardly express them.

So I spent most of my early days in a corner with my keyboard, directing my chorus line of stuffed animals. I'd also steal stacks of loose paper from my mom's home office printer, fold them in half to form a booklet, and would fill them up, pages and pages, with comics, short stories, drawings, poetry, and lyrics.

While my mother was encouraging of my big recording artist and published author dreams, both my parents preferred I err on the side of safety. It's easier for a person with a disability to succeed on a straight and narrow path rather than forge their own, but those who move mountains and change the world very rarely play it safe.

Finding Purpose

I went to the best public college in my state, University of North Carolina, to study business, telling my dad and myself I was going to be an accountant. Wanting to mix music with being a college nerd, I joined the Glee Club, which was probably the worst possible thing for my accounting career. Being actively involved in music opened me up in a big way. I could express myself musically while being in a social setting. Sharing my talent with others, I felt things like pride and confidence, feelings I hadn't felt before in social situations.

This propelled me to form my own acapella music group on campus. I had no idea how to start one on my own, so I posted ads in forums and hung flyers.

Who knew over fifty people would audition? As my music ensemble grew in prominence, I began to put on my own solo sideshow. On Saturdays, I'd play my dormitory's community piano for drunk coeds looking to continue hanging after a big party. These piano nights grew so popular that I began to book gigs around town.

Music now fueling my confidence, I mentioned to an advisor my dreams of pursuing music and writing in New York City. "So do it," he said. Such simple yet most profound advice. And, so I did. Despite my parents' and my own fears, it wasn't long before I was studying music at New York University. I raised just enough money for the bus ticket and a few nights camping out at a YMCA, but it was certainly one of my best life gambles.

I could get anywhere I wanted through the convenient metro system for less than two dollars! Sure beat the limitations I faced with having to beg my parents to drive me everywhere, or waiting two hours for a bus, and another forty five minutes for a bus transfer in the hot sun or cold winter. Floating freely in a constant stream of musicians, writers, oddballs, rich yuppies, and folks with varying degrees of disability who didn't think twice about them, all hustling towards greatness, was exactly what I needed.

After finishing up at NYU, I landed a job working for the United States Army Corps of Engineers as a program assistant. Sitting behind the desk clicking away, my body vibrated for that pride and that confidence I felt in sharing my creative talents. Times were tough at the Corps. I learned that being socially awkward due to a disability can cause cliquish behavior in workplace adults as well. And hammering around a self-advocacy bull horn of "accept me!" was tough for a girl who appeared to have all the fixings for a socially well-adjusted human.

One day, naturally, I got fed up with the lack of music and creativity in my life. I took a few days off work so a friend and I could play guitar/vocal sets at a few local bars down in Texas during SXSW, a large annual music festival in the region. Before going, I wrote a cold-email to about ten record label agents asking them if they'd be at the festival and to come to one of my performances. No one responded. We went anyway. An agent showed up, and not long after, I signed a recording contract.

Nowadays

Ten years later, I am now an award-nominated recording artist recognized by the Grammys. I have a fancy management team and my own studio, am a published author with an agent, and I travel the world for my art. I've released music with Sony, Universal, and Warner Music, have had music debut on international dance charts with streams in the millions, have heard my songs played on the radio, and seen my music featured in TV and film. I've had the opportunity to work with some of the biggest names in the industry, from opening for Patti Labelle, to collaborating on a song with Snoop

Dogg, to support from DJs like Armin van Buuren and Markus Schulz.

It took hard work and ingenuity, as I have to run ten times as long to get to the same destination as my sighted peers. But by working hard, thinking outside the box, and with stark determination, these things are like air to those who aren't born with the luxury of monotony.

I'm most proud that I've been able to use my platform to help raise the visibility of persons with disabilities in mainstream media, as well as educate those who would otherwise have no idea of the social stigmas the disability community deals with every day. I spread this message so that when an eight year old girl, who feels outcast because of her sight impairments or any other disability, can turn on the television, see herself prominently represented and think, "I can definitely be me someday!"

Follow Lachi's success at:

Facebook: www.facebook.com/lachimusic
Twitter: @lachimusic
Instagram: @lachimusic

UK born Chris Skelley found his wings and fought his way to the top

Sometimes it's the dark periods of our life that give us the determination to get back up and forge ahead with our dreams. Chris has definitely found this to be the case, and his drive has led him to become a champion in his field. Chris' story shows that adopting a fighting spirit can lead us to a level that may not have been in our vision without the push of the challenge...

Photo description: Chris Skelley facing forward wearing his Great Britain Judo top, in front of British Judo sign.

Hi, my name is Chris Skelley. I am a Paralympic Judo athlete. I was born on 09/07/93 so that makes me middle aged for an athlete, which is quite scary. I was born in Nottingham, UK, but I moved to Hull when I was really young and lived most of the rest of my life in Hull until I moved to Walsall in 2013.

I started Rugby and Judo at the age of five. My parents got me into sport because they wanted me to socialise with other people, they wanted me to make sure I progressed in society and didn't get identified as a person with hearing problems.

My hearing problems have lasted throughout my whole life so my mum and dad wanted to make sure I worked hard at socialising and interacting with people. And I carried Rugby and Judo alongside each other. I used to go to school and then in the evenings I used to do my sport. It kept me off the street corners and kept me on the straight and narrow and really gave me a structured life, which I loved.

I left school at 16. I had good grades – I had struggled at school because I had really bad dyslexia and hearing problems and I started to notice that my sight was struggling a little bit but I just thought, you know, I needed glasses. Then I left school and trained to be a mechanic.

Between ages 16 and 20 was the worst time in my life because I really struggled with my eyes – they got a lot worse with the light, with sight and vision, and I struggled to see in the dark. I started to become really reactive to light. I really struggled with depth perception and it kind of freaked me out a bit.

There were no answers to what was happening to me, so in this part of my life I lost my job and my driving and everything kind of left my hands. I was really struggling and the only constant thing in my life was Judo. Judo took me out of that dark part in my life and really helped me through that difficult period – because I had no answers.

None of the doctors in England could help me with getting a diagnosis. So I went over to America. I started with a clean sheet over there. I was very lucky to have a private sponsor who got me over there to get me a diagnosis. I came back here and with further tests found out that I had ocular albinism. Apparently I've always had it but there was no diagnosing me when I was really young. I've always struggled with my eyes but no one told me until I got to America, or when I came back here, to talk to some private doctors. From that I got classified to be a visually impaired Judo fighter.

So when one door closed (my job and my driving) another one opened with Judo. In 2013 I got offered a place at the British Judo Centre for Excellence to train and travel around the world and become a full time Judo athlete. That was a really special time in my life, because everything was lost and I had no other option - I had no one to point me in the right direction - but I felt I could do it as a job and it took off from there.

Then, in 2015, two years into my training at the Centre, I had one of my worst injuries I have had so far (touch wood). I was in Grimsby one night with my coach, Ian Johns, and I dislocated my hip. At that point it got really dark in my life; it was a really dark moment because my career nearly ended there and then. I was lying on the mat crying and screaming. I was trying to qualify for Rio 2016 and I wasn't in a very good position; I was quite low down in the world ranking list and I had to go and fight in Korea which was six weeks later. I got the dislocated hip put back in after about six hours of waiting on the judo mat for an ambulance to come. Then I had another operation two or three weeks later. Three weeks after that I was in Korea fighting.

So that was a really dark period again in my life. Not only because a few years before that I had lost everything, and then gained it back because of Judo, but then I nearly lost it again. And it really made me want to medal at the World Games in Korea.

I medalled at a few tournaments, which put me in a tremendous place for qualifying for Rio, which I did. The preparation for Rio was really good with no injuries. Sadly, Rio wasn't my time: I didn't medal. This was a really down period again, a really dark period; because I really wanted to medal and have a success in everything I did. It only made me stronger and want to carry on.

After that in 2017 I got back on the horse, you know, carried on riding – like Joe Mallon. I had one of my highest career highlights, which was winning the European Championships in Walsall. This was really special to me because my mum, my dad, my sister and my friends were there. So everyone saw the most important day so far in my career.

Leading into Tokyo in 2018 I had a good summer. I got a World bronze medal and in 2019 I became world number one – which was another career highlight. So in the last four years I've grown up a lot and my career has flourished, I think you would say. I've had some really good results and now, hopefully, I have a good chance of getting a medal in the Tokyo Paralympic Games.

Preparations leading to Tokyo have been really good. Last year was my best year yet because every competition I went to I medalled at. Last year I got: two gold, two silver and two bronze medals which I'm really pleased about. I had a great block of months getting myself bigger and stronger and I'm still doing that now as I enter into the the final push for Tokyo. Hopefully, I can carry on with good preparation and move forward.

It's very good to currently be ranked world number one, especially going into Tokyo, but everyone who does Judo knows that ranking doesn't matter, especially on the day. As long as I get my preparations right leading to Tokyo I'm not bothered where I'm ranked. I just want to make sure I put a good performance in when I fight.

Off the mat I am an ambassador for a charity in Swindon called Phoenix Enterprises which helps people get back into work. I'm also an ambassador back in Hull for a charity called Disability Sport Humber which helps people get into sport with a disability and helps them raise money and awareness around the Shropshire area.

I am going to go back to college after the Paralympics and train to be a level 3 counsellor. I'm a keen pork pie enthusiast - I love my pork pies, which my nutritionist is not happy about. I also love a good quiz. Some of the lads from the Judo team have set up a quiz team on a Tuesday night, so I like to try and take my mind away from Judo when I'm not doing it.

It's important to have a separate part of your life to be a bit more of a person outside of Judo. I'm also a godfather which I'm really pleased about. So, you know, I'm everywhere. I'm here, there and everywhere. I'm like a butterfly.

Family has played an important role in my life. They have supported me. My mum has been there since day one of Judo, and my dad has too, and my sisters, who all just support me in my journey. Recently, in the last few years, I've had more help from family and friends. I also have a serious girlfriend who is a Paralympic tennis player, so she understands the pressures of sport and that's really nice to have that support from her as well. And I have a great group of friends. I'm very lucky to have a good support network around me and I'm very, very happy.

Follow Chris to see how he gets on in Tokyo at...

Facebook: www.facebook.com/Hulls-Champion-Christopher-Skelley-326233737712289/
Twitter: @BritishJudo and @ChristopherSke2
Instagram: @britishjudo and @christopher.skelley
LinkedIn: www.linkedin.com/company/british-judo-association/

Nicole from Detroit, USA, removed the limits imposed on her by others, and now she's limitless in her dreams

It's easy to allow the fears of others to tarnish our reality, especially when filled with negative and limiting concepts as a child. But as Nicole discovered, learning to believe in ourselves can set us free, and when we are free to believe, anything is possible...it is!

Here, Nicole tells her journey from restriction to inspiration...

Photo description: Nicole smiling and facing the camera, outside with house and greenery behind her.

Grab your favorite snack, a box of tissues, and make yourself comfortable, because you're about to go on an adventure! The adventure of the life of Nicole Kada. Are you ready? Here it goes in 3, 2, 1!

My name is Nicole and I am currently 24 years old. I am a young lady from Detroit, Michigan, in the United States. I have 3 siblings all younger than me, I'm Middle Eastern, have a bachelor's degree, am a YouTuber, love to travel, and - best of all - I am legally blind!

I was born with Leber's Congenital Amaurosis, or LCA for short. This is an eye disorder that affects the retina, which is the part of the eye that allows for sight. It's typically a degenerative disorder, so I had a great deal of eyesight as a kid, but it has worsened as I've gotten older. Now, I am only able to see light, dark, shapes, shadows, and outlines.

My parents are Iraqi, along with the majority of the rest of my family members. However, I was born in America. The Middle Eastern background played a significant role in shaping me to be the person that I am today. It has caused me the most pain and brought me the greatest successes simultaneously.

My family raised me Catholic. My grandparents on my dad's side, along with some of my dad's sisters and nieces lived with us for many years of my early childhood. Because of being Catholic and living with many foreigners, I faced many challenges. In Middle Eastern culture those with disabilities are looked down on and treated like they're incapable of taking care of themselves and won't amount to anything. Sometimes, I felt like I was treated as if I were helpless. Because my grandma was so religious and had an old mindset from back home, I felt less human because of her friend group and the elderly family members that would come over. I constantly had to hear how they were sorry for me, but that I'm such a bright kid. I had to hear how they hoped for a cure for me. I had to hear things like how would I get married and have children of my own in the future? Because of all the pity and making me feel helpless, I accepted the pity and let myself be that "poor blind helpless person".

In school, I struggled to make and keep friends. I was placed in a classroom for the blind for the majority of elementary school, until the program got shut down and then I was placed in regular classes in my hometown. From kindergarten to my senior year of high school, I attended 7 schools. Every time I made a friend, I would leave that school. Also, I struggled to make friends, because my parents told me to keep my friends at school. The only time I had friends over was if they were also middle eastern. Not only that, but they kept me from attending certain field trips and going camping, out of fear that something terrible would happen to me. I completely understand the fear now but, as a kid, that destroyed me. My peers were having sleep-overs and doing cool things together, while I was spending my time outside of school alone, unless I was with siblings, or another Middle Eastern person.

At school, I was bullied. At home, I thought about how I would never be anything in the future. Nobody would want to be with me. By 8th grade, I was miserable no matter where I was at. I had so many journal entries written about hating my life and how I'd be better off dead. These entries continued until I was 17, which is the time when I broke out of my depression and started finding my happiness.

I finally went to a summer camp for the blind and met others like myself. I was away from my parents long enough to realize that I didn't need them to do everything for me in order for me to survive. I was away long enough to know that blind people are capable of being independent. For so long, I craved independence and now I had it. I had it and I never let go of it after I had a hold of it!

The next year I started college. I attended three different colleges: this was for two reasons. The first being the lack of services provided at the first two colleges, and the second reason being that I majored in things that I didn't have a passion for, because I allowed others to discourage me from following my dreams. Eventually, I stopped listening to others and I became a science major. Science was my passion and I didn't care how visual it was, I was going to do it and I did! I received my bachelor's in Nutrition and Food Science. I took and aced visual classes like math, biology, and even organic chemistry. I met with tutors/ scribes, went to professors' office hours, and required extra time on exams/assignments, but all that matters is that I did it! I got my bachelor's and now I'm going to continue my education to become a Registered Dietitian - something that will be difficult as a blind person, but I will make it happen.

I've only been happy for about 7 years now, but one of the most valuable lessons I've learned is loving and accepting myself. After that camp in 2013, I found my happiness. Instead of looking for pity, I make blind jokes constantly. Instead of letting others tell me what I can or can't do, I show them what I *will* do. Even if it takes me a longer time to accomplish something compared to my sighted peers, if it means making my dreams come true, I will do it. However, it takes loving yourself to reach that positive and determined mindset. Because when you love yourself, no level of negativity will discourage you. When you love yourself, your confidence speaks so loudly that you attract the things you want, sometimes even without having to seek them. For example, one of my goals is to inspire others and without looking for an opportunity to inspire, I was presented with the opportunity to write this.

When you are confident, you attract the things you want and the negative things quietly start disappearing. You begin to surround yourself with like-minded people, experience life-changing events, and do things you never thought you could. For example, I started doing some traveling and also became a YouTuber; both things I was afraid to do but, because of my level of confidence, I have been able to step out of my comfort zone and do anything I put my mind to. To the outside, my blindness is a disability but, to me, it is my ability. I know many sighted people who place limits on themselves and, to me, *that* is a disability. Remove limits and you are automatically able!

Follow Nicole's flourishing career on social media at;

YouTube: search for channel Nicole Kada
Facebook: www.facebook.com/BlindBossEntertainment
Twitter: @blind_boss
Instagram: @blinding_beauty14

British Elliot is proud that, with his willingness to accept guidance, he is set for success at the Paralympics

Sometimes it takes being sent off-course to rediscover what we are truly passionate about, and to allow ourselves to be supported back to where we need to be. Elliot has found that accepting help from his family and teammates, has helped him reach the heights that he always dreamed of…

Photo description: Elliot Stewart facing forward wearing his Great Britain Judo top, in front of British Judo sign.

My name is Elliot Stewart, I was born on the 22nd February 1988 and I am an under 90kg Para-athlete heading for the Tokyo Paralympic Games.

For a little bit of back story: I did Judo from a young age, my dad was at the 1988 Seoul Games and won a bronze medal. That was the year I was born, so I was basically born into Judo and have done Judo for most of my life. I had quite a successful cadet career and quite a successful junior career. I trained hard, and worked hard, and Judo was pretty much everything I did.

When I got to about 20 years old, I moved countries over to Hong Kong. I started up my own Judo club there. It was a successful club; I was coaching and still training and doing a bit of Judo myself. Whilst in Hong Kong I started a family: I had two kids and then came back to the UK with my children so that they could be educated here. I then had another child and got married. So, at the age of 25, I was married with three kids.

I decided to go to University and become a PE teacher. I attended Wolverhampton University doing a Physical Education course. Year one and year two were great – I really enjoyed it.

In year three, when I was 27, the final year of my course, I started struggling to see what was on the board. I thought it was just my eyes deteriorating; I was getting a bit older. I went to the opticians and they gave me some glasses. They worked for a little bit but then the month after I had to go back again to get them changed and change my prescription. I did this about three or four months in a row. On the fourth month they said that I might have a condition called keratoconus, which is where my cornea is in a cone shape.

Surprisingly, it is actually quite common in a really mild form but I went to hospital to get it checked. They said that my cornea had morphed quite a lot, so I had to have an operation. I decided to have the operation done privately, because it was such a long wait on the NHS; they said it was a five month wait and within that five months I might have to have a corneal transplant, which I didn't want to have. All my family (my brothers, my wife, my wife's family) put together, they all chipped in some money for me to have my eyes done. Both my eyes have cross linking on both, so the operation was to stop the morph on my cornea and to keep the vision that I had currently.

Just to explain my vision: it varies day to day, it is basically like looking through tears, or the bottom of a glass; where everything is blurred and you can't focus on anything, you just can't focus. So nothing is ever clear. That is the vision that I have been able to get used to over the last three years. I had the operation. (Cross linking you are basically staying awake and they numb your eyes and they use vitamin D and laser treatment to harden the cornea).

The recovery was a lot worse than the actual operation. It took me two weeks to recover, three days with my eyes tightly shut. Again I was around my family, around my kids, so that was really difficult - them knowing what was happening to me and seeing me going from being with vision to losing my vision. That was a really difficult time. My wife was there helping me through all the tough times, and without them I don't think I would have been able to do it.

After I had the operation, I finished my university course, luckily, and they really accommodated for me. They understood my situation and they helped me out. I was able to use voice notes for all my exams, all my coursework, my dissertation and presentations that I had to do. I passed my degree, which I am really proud of because I didn't think I was going to be able to do it with the vision that I had at the time and the operation going ahead.

After I had finished that I didn't feel like there was anything left. I was working in schools at the time, teaching Judo whilst I was at university. Because of my vision problem they had taken my driving licence off me and I wasn't able to work anymore. I felt like I wasn't able to look after my family because I didn't have a job. I didn't think I would be able to get another job with my vision because I always thought 'why would you want someone who has a visual impairment when you could pick someone who has totally fine sight compared to me?'

Two or three weeks after my operation I was pretty down, I had given up really. Then, through Judo, yet again, I found out about the visually impaired team, and found out about the Paralympics and that they had quite a strong team at the British Judo Centre of Excellence. I went back to Judo, after speaking to Denny Roberts and British Judo Paralympic Head Coach, Ian Johns, about it. They were really keen to get me tested, get my vision tested, to see if I qualified to be a para-athlete and luckily I did.

I had my operation in April, and in August I was in my first event, which was the European Championships. That was my first real big event in six years and since then I have been back on the programme. I have been training hard and I'm back at Judo with my new set of goals and new achievements to get, like: the World championships, European Championship and the Paralympics.

So far I've been in the system for just coming up to three years now and I have got two world bronze medals and a European bronze medal. So I am achieving those goals, training hard and back doing the sport that I love. Those days where I gave up and didn't think I would be able to do anything - I wanted to but I didn't think I could - those days are behind me now. With the athletes around me, and the rest of the team, they've taught me how to be a VI athlete and how to be a visually impaired member of the community.

It was difficult for me to adapt from being fully sighted to being visually impaired, because there are a lot of things that I still try and do like I did when I was sighted. I had a lot of time being sighted, luckily. Now I struggle getting my head around doing things differently and accommodating for my vision. With athletes around me, (the whole of the VI team; Jack Hodgson, Chris Skelley, Evan Molloy and Dan Powell, all of them) they have helped me be visually impaired because they have been visually impaired a lot longer than me.

Even though I am the oldest person on the team, in some ways I guide the team and I'm an older brother to the team, I still rely on them a lot to help me get through everyday life because they are a lot more experienced in being visually impaired than me. With that network of people around me; my family, the VI team, the coaches around the Centre, it gives me the confidence to try and do anything I need to do, or at least ask for help to accomplish the easier tasks.

Now, my sole goal is for the Tokyo Paralympics - to try and medal and be on that rostrum at the Games. The way things are going - training is going well, preparations are going well, and recent competitions have been going well - it's looking good at the minute.

Follow Elliot's progress:

Facebook: www.facebook.com/britishjudo and www. facebook.com/ElliotJudoStewart
Twitter: @BritishJudo and @ElliotJudo
Instagram: @britishjudo and @ElliotJudo
LinkedIn: www.linkedin.com/company/british-judo-association

James from Scotland, UK, learned to love himself through sight loss, and now lives a full life of no regrets

James didn't need perfect sight to see a world philosophy that would set him up for life.

As his vision diminished, James' love for himself grew, and holding the wise perspective that our own perception of ourselves can sometimes be the biggest hurdle to overcome has left him determined to live life to the full...

Photo description: James Laird standing outside with rock formation behind him, wearing a SuperDry top and vision assistance technological glasses from OrCam.

To those who read this, my name is James Laird, and this is my tale. Across my lifetime I have combated and thrived through a sight loss condition known as Retinitus Pigmentosa (RP). This condition means that my sight slowly deteriorates across my lifetime to an unknown end point. Despite this, I've endeavoured to live my life to its fullest capacity. If I had to have a life motto it would be that I aim to live a life without regrets. I have often found – in literature, pop culture and from the voices of others – that it isn't the choices we make that we regret, it's the choices we don't. Thus, I have taken every opportunity, seized upon every chance, and tried to make the most from whatever has been put in front of me.

At an early age I was told that my sight would be temporary. At the time I was unable to fully grasp what this meant; though I do remember one event that brought some sobriety to my pre-teen mind. It was the moment I asked my mother if this meant my dream to become a racing driver was over. While she hid it well, the emotional backlash from my words was not lost upon me. I knew things were going to change, I just didn't realise in what way. Over the coming years I thought deeply on my feelings, and I concluded I had a choice. I could succumb to the situation, allow my impairment to dictate to me what I would and wouldn't do, how I would and wouldn't live, and what I would and wouldn't experience – or I could make the most of the time I had.

When put in such a fashion the choice was easy to make, and from then until now I have never looked back. So, what are my experiences with sight loss? That is harder to answer than first thought. My life is a life experienced through the lens of sight loss. My perceptions, opinions and attitudes have all formed around this diminishing sense. It then becomes a matter of which experiences in a life full of adventure I wish to share – a 'top moments' if you will.

I could talk about my experiences travelling the world; visiting places like China, California, Thailand and Egypt. I could mention my time swimming at the sixth best beach in the world, scuba-diving with dolphins and whale sharks, or even riding – and crashing – a quad bike in the desert. I could even enlighten you all to my plight of surviving homelessness, persecution, starvation and being hunted by the authorities, while attempting to live in one of the twenty-three nations I was lucky enough to travel to...but I think I will be saving those stories for another time. Instead I want to talk about my experiences coming to terms with the notion that I am worthy of love.

I am the first to admit that, for a long time, I struggled with reconciling the idea that someone wouldn't be 'settling' for me. I saw my impairment as something hideous, as a horrible deterrent that would push others away, so only those who were willing to 'settle' would accept me. I felt pitiable, that I was somehow... lesser than those around me. I battled with this for a long time, even going as far as refusing to accept a date with a woman I had 'taken a fancy to' out of the belief that I was unworthy of her. Self-sacrificial male that I was, I had somehow convinced myself this was a noble act. By the time I was sixteen I had yet to realise that I was more than a single aspect; that if someone else were to refuse me for who I am then I was better off without them. As I pondered the meaning of the universe – which if you ask any teenager is centred around themselves – I steadily concluded that I had more to offer a partner than my 'lack of vision.' I was smart, funny, stubborn – though I prefer to say determined or tenacious – and if given the right assistance from a rather talented family member, handsome in my own right.

While I perhaps couldn't offer to drive my potential date to the movies after getting a bite to eat, I could still provide them with happiness. The world now, in my own opinion, is fantastic at sapping the joy from experiences. The youthful ignorance fades away to reveal a world that, if given half a chance, would take away your stolen moments of happiness. I learned that I had to 'make' my own happiness. That in the same way I would regret letting choices, chances and opportunities slip by; I could not rely on happiness finding me. I would go out and find it, and it was up to me to make of it what I could.

I realised that I was a person with faults but also merits, and that my opinion mattered as much as anyone else's – simply because it was my opinion. I had equal standing in the world - I had a more visceral 'imperfection' than others but at least mine was on the outside. Others may have theirs hidden away, but we all have them; it just so happens that mine is more – rather ironically if you think about it – visible.

Love came to me in many shapes, styles and formats. I have a family that loves me, faults and all. Friends who would stand at my back in a fight, pick me up when I'm down, ask for my advice, and who would trust me with their infant child. I am loved. I just needed to look beyond my own prejudice to see it. I may be blind, but I have a world view I would never change. I am who I am because I have lived my life through my experiences with sight loss. My attitudes, opinions, thoughts, behaviours are sculpted by the life that I've lived. I am sight loss. I am me.

Follow James on social media here:

Facebook: www.facebook.com/james.laird.9216
Instagram: @jclaird94

Jono from Australia found his identity within his passion, and wants you to know that this is possible for anyone, despite what life throws at you

Jono proudly recounts the years that it took for his life to travel 'full circle' right back to where he started; dreams of being an elite athlete. As Jono says, finding our passion and then putting our every hard effort into making it happen, despite what others might say, is the only way to achieve our goals...

My name is Jonathan Goerlach, dob 07/11/1982, currently 37 years old (at time of writing this) and I was born in a town called Nowra on the south coast in New South Wales, which is about 2 and a half hours south of Sydney. I have 4 siblings and was raised by a single mum. My mum is Marianne, my elder brother is Ben, my elder sister Katy, and my two younger sisters are Erin and Stephanie.

I've had hearing impairment my whole life. I was diagnosed at about age 3 and shortly after that I started wearing hearing aids. So, for the first probably third of my life, I was the hearing impaired kid and wore hearing aids all throughout primary school and some of high school. High school was pretty brutal - I was singled out and bullied quite a bit early on, just because I was seen as different, and that led to me choosing not to wear hearing aids for much of high school. That meant I missed out a lot in class, as I didn't hear what the teachers were saying, but the bullying didn't stop, I was still always seen as different.

I was very passionate about sport from an early age, as far back as I can remember. My dad was always into sport, and my grandad. I didn't have a relationship with my dad – my parents broke up when I was about 4 – so my grandad, Alan, he was pretty much my father figure (until he passed away in November 2019). He was my best mate as well and, as he was very passionate about sport, I learnt a lot about sport through him. All through school I was passionate about all sports, and was quite good at a lot of them too, with a natural talent. Sport, especially through high school, was the one escape that I had from bullying and from feeling different.

I started playing tennis from about age 8 and I played that religiously for about 10 years. If I wasn't on a tennis court I was up at the school which was across the road from the house I grew up in, and I'd be up there for hours hitting the ball against the wall - or up at my grandparents' house doing the same thing. Once the school bell rang I would head straight to the tennis court - I'd have my racket with me all day at school and head straight to training. It was one escape. It was my passion, it gave me a focus, it gave me a lot of drive; I was treated as an equal rather than being a hearing impaired kid or being the different kid, it was a place I was treated with respect for my ability rather than having a disability.

About age 15, I had a visit from an aunty (my dad's sister) whom I hadn't seen for years. She visited with my cousins and I remember her vision wasn't very good, but I didn't understand what that was at the time. Mum tells me they were having a cup of tea and she was telling stories about me running into things or not being able to find things. I'd had my eyes tested a few years earlier and the optometrist had told me it wasn't anything to worry about, but my aunty, who knew that I was also hearing impaired, suggested to my mum that maybe I needed to get tested for a condition called Usher Syndrome, which is the condition that my aunty had been diagnosed with only a few years earlier. She was also hearing impaired and she found out that she had the vision impairment side of things too, with RP (Retinitis Pigmentosa). So that visit from my aunty prompted my mum to take me down to a local optometrist and they had the facilities to do the peripheral field testing and, even twenty years on, I still remember everything about that appointment.

I remember waiting beforehand to go in. The optometrist was in the local shopping centre where my mum had worked for many years prior to that. The shopping centre had shut down and we were the last appointment to go in. We went in and had the field test done; my grandad was there with me, and I still vividly remember afterwards in the waiting room when the optometrist brought out the results and spoke to my mum and my grandad about them. He showed us the spherical graph, with the black circle on the outside and the white in the middle, which is all you can see with your peripheral vision if you have RP. I remember my mum being upset and I knew something wasn't right.

At that stage it wasn't confirmed as Usher Syndrome, but it was confirmed when I saw a geneticist a couple of weeks later. The optometrist explained that I may go blind one day and, as a 15 year old kid who still had some vision, that was confusing. But knowing what being blind meant made me feel a bit numb at the time, and I didn't know what to expect.

Of all the things you might think of - all the questions that you might ask when told you would potentially be blind one day - they weren't questions like: 'Am I going to be able to have a proper job?'; 'Am I going to be able to have a wife and raise children?'; 'Am I going to do all the normal things that people do?'. The only question I had for my optometrist was: 'Am I going to be able to play tennis?'. I was so passionate about tennis and about sport and that was all I cared about at that age. That was what gave me my identity. That was my purpose. So when I got told I wasn't going to be able to see my first thought was that I wasn't going to be able to play tennis. And that was a bit of a shock.

From that point on I didn't really tell anyone about it; it was only my family that knew. So for the last few years of high school I pretty much flopped - I just wasn't engaged in it. I still did everything to do with sport, but I got to a point, when I was 18, where I got sick of playing sport, because I couldn't compete with everyone anymore. It wasn't a level playing field. My vision was getting worse. I learnt that my night vision was an issue with RP and that training at nighttime with tennis or ARF (Australian Rules Football) was all too difficult. I gave up playing sport and gave up my passion.

My older brother and sister were living and working in Sydney, so I decided to move up there and try something new, having to learn to live with being legally blind. Back in 1998 the internet was still pretty new; it hadn't been about that long. There was definitely no social media, no smartphones, any of that. There were no support networks. I wasn't getting any professional support from anyone who knew what to expect, or from anyone who knew what it was like to live with a degenerative vision impairment. I didn't know anyone with the condition apart from my aunty, but we weren't really in contact at that stage. I didn't know anyone else who had a vision impairment, let alone Usher Syndrome. I didn't have anyone to talk to. I was alone and I was the only person I knew with this syndrome so I ended up just keeping it to myself and just trying to deal with it.

It felt as though I had no choice but to just bottle it up, push it down and go on with things as if I was still okay. So for several years, living in Sydney, I was going from job to job and, looking back on it, I was in denial, and that meant there was ongoing trauma under the surface, with me not dealing with this problem that was continuing to grow.

Through those years (between 18/19 years old and 25/26) I had no identity because I had no purpose. I wasn't playing sport, I wasn't studying or doing anything that I was passionate about. I was just trying to fit into society and fit in with my social groups. I was out partying every weekend, taking recreational drugs, just being a single young person - travelling a lot and still experiencing culture in different parts of the world - but I was just trying to do what all the young people were doing at that age: trying to fit in, and not be seen as different like I was in high school.

I had a real big reality check at about age 26/27. My GP had been hassling me to prepare for the fact that my vision was probably getting worse and that I needed to prepare for life potentially being blind one day. I hadn't been doing that and he urged me to go and get my eyes tested again. It had been almost ten years roughly since I had had my eyes tested and so, sure enough, I got a referral and it was out of one of the hospitals in Sydney. That was in itself a traumatic day. It was two hours travel to this hospital and it was a six hour process from when I got there: getting the eye drops, getting all the nurses to do all their checks first and then sitting in the waiting room for another hour and a half with dozens of older people. It was a really depressing environment to be in. Eventually, when it was my turn to see the ophthalmologist, I had about 5 minutes with him and all he told me was, 'Oh yeah, you have Retinal Pigmentosa and this is how bad your eyesight is now'.

There was no advice, no information. I asked if there was any cure or anything like that happening and he said, 'No, nothing like that happening. Maybe in 10 years'. And that was it, I was just left with the reality and this updated information which told me that my eyes were getting a lot worse and that I was well on the way to being blind. My GP was right, I hadn't prepared for it and I was still trying to process what it all meant for me. At that time I went into a downward spiral.

I still remember my first anxiety attack, sitting with a big group of friends. It was after a big night out and we were all sitting in a café having breakfast and it just hit me. I don't know why, I don't know what caused it. I just had this overwhelming negative feeling come over me and I started to panic and get the sweats. I just literally stood up and walked out. I didn't even say anything to anyone, which was probably weird to everyone. I just walked out of the café and raced home and locked myself in my room. It was horrible.

That happened more times and I didn't know what it was. It was all new and I think that came off the back of being a bit depressed and not knowing that I was depressed. It took me about six months of not hanging out with my mates, and not being the same person that I was, until my mum noticed what was going on and said I needed to go and see someone. My same GP referred me to a psychologist, the same one I'm still seeing now - I've been seeing her for 12 years now and she's amazing. I'm so glad that I have been able to work with someone on my mental distress. That was the very starting point of changing my life around. I had to learn what mental distress was and I had to learn that I could regain charge of my life and set myself on the right course. Being a visibly impaired person, your family and friends are very protective over you and can shelter you too much. I allowed that behaviour to the point where there were things like when I was 21 I said that I would like to go and live overseas, and they said that would be too hard for me, and that I wouldn't be able to get a job. I believed what they were saying, and it was an example of times where people would make decisions for me and I didn't have the confidence or courage to say: 'No. I can do this', because I didn't know if I could.

With the psychologist I learnt to reclaim my independence and make decisions for myself. For example, when I was 4 years old I nearly drowned in my dad's backyard pool and that traumatic experience meant that for the next nearly 24 years I never went near water. I never learnt to swim. I didn't participate in carnivals at school. I missed out on many events and opportunities with friends and family over the years because I avoided water.

One of the things I challenged myself to do was to learn to swim. As a 27 year old I attended swimming classes and I learnt to go and find things that I enjoyed again. I had spent so many years doing things to fit in with other people but I wasn't doing anything for myself. And one of those things was to start playing sport again. My eyesight was definitely a lot worse than when I stopped playing sport. I needed to go and do something I enjoyed and that I loved. It wasn't tennis; I hadn't picked a racket up in years, because it scared me to think I wouldn't be able to play tennis like I used to.

I was living in Sydney and I had always been interested in rowing, so I joined a rowing club. It was the first sport that I engaged in and I did that for about 18 months and really enjoyed it. This was at the same time that I was learning to swim. So, interestingly, I was learning to swim but I was also out on a boat. Most of our training would be at 5am, when the water was flattest and smoothest, which was also when it was pitch black for at least the first half, if not most, of the training session. So, you know, you're out on the water, you can't swim, you're nervous as hell, and you're learning this new technique which is quite technical and hard, and it was pitch black and I couldn't see anything.

Then one of the other challenges I set myself was going overseas and living in another country, which is something I was told I wasn't capable of, so I saved my money and spent a year working it all out. I got my visa for the Netherlands and booked a one way ticket. I didn't book a return flight and I just said: 'I'm going'. Aged 28 I travelled for a few months through Europe.

Before arriving in Amsterdam, I went to the Lake District in Northern England and met with about six other people of a similar age at the time who also had RP. It was the first time I had met anyone with RP of a similar age who I could relate to. It was a very significant moment in my life to have that opportunity to share my story with others who all had very similar stories and just spend three or four days hanging out and having a beer and spending time with each other - just essentially knowing that we weren't alone. One of the people who was at that event was Yvette; that's how we became friends and we're still friends today. That in itself was a really life changing moment.

I ended up living in Amsterdam for about 18 months. The newfound confidence and attitude that I had developed at home before I left, was enabling me to take risks; taking on opportunities and not thinking so much about what it would mean if I did it. I hadn't ridden a bike for over 10 years, but I spent over two thirds of my time in Amsterdam riding a bike all over the city. It was amazing, something so simple and I was able to reclaim my independence. I had a couple of close mates from Australia that were living there too, and it was really good to have them there, but essentially I was there on my own to meet new people and try new things. That was a real pivotal moment in my life that set me on this path that I find myself on now.

It was around 18 months I was there and it was around 2011, just before I turned 30, when I decided to move back to Australia. Apart from the visa ending, the main reason to move home was because when I was living in Amsterdam I didn't continue with my rowing. I did get back into my running, and I joined the athletics club there, and whilst I did that I came across an article on the internet about the Paralympic Games - a year later the London 2012 games would be held - I thought maybe I should see if I was eligible to compete. It was the first time I had actually even thought about it. I didn't think my eyesight would be bad enough to be eligible to be classified to compete in para sports.

I contacted my national Paralympic committee back home and sent them my latest visual results and they said that I was eligible. I didn't have enough time to prepare for London; I needed several years to train in any sport really let alone running. But I had seen a press release saying that Triathlon had been accepted into the Paralympics, in Rio 2016. And it was the first time Triathlon had been accepted in the games.

I had loved watching Triathlon as a kid - although I couldn't swim and avoided the water as a kid I really appreciated how fit they were. So that was it. I said, 'okay, it's 2011. I've got 5 years to train and see if I can do this and achieve this goal of becoming an elite athlete'. My life changed from the moment I set myself that goal.

In 2015 I had a major setback. Those of you who know para-sports or Paralympic sports know that there are several disability types in a sport and because of that it is impossible to have a medal event at a Paralympic Games for every single disability type in every single sport. So there is a quota on the amount of sports and then within each sport there is a quota of medal events that that sport will have that they need to choose to disperse amongst the categories. So, unfortunately for me, for our sport we were given a quota of 3 medal events per gender and, at the time, we had five different disability categories, so two categories had to miss out.

I was told that I didn't have a medal event, and that was a huge set back, not only that I wasn't going to have the opportunity to go to Rio but also for funding.

I was being funded by my national federation and it is an expensive sport, when you're travelling all over the world, and especially when you have to race with a guide. In triathlon I need to race with a sighted guide. We swim together, ride a tandem bike and we run together too. So I needed to cover their costs also. Having no Rio event meant that I no longer received funding support because I was no longer on a pathway to the Games. So the next couple of years were really, really tough and I wasn't sure I was going to stay in the sport. I was shattered that I couldn't achieve the goal that I had set out to achieve and I wasn't sure if I was going to continue onto the Tokyo Paralympic Games; it was a long way away and the sport was going to continue getting better and more competitive. Also I didn't know if I was going to be good enough, and I didn't know if I could continue to afford to pay for two people to keep travelling all over the world to keep racing and gaining ranking points, as it is just a big process.

But I just decided to take the risk and stick with my passion. That was advice that was given to me very early on back in 2012 when I took part in an Australian Paralympic Committee talent search day. When I got back from Amsterdam I went and did that to see if I had good ability in any sport. The advice I was given that day was whichever sport you decide to go with make sure it is one you are passionate about, because if you pick a sport that is an easier way to get into a Paralympic games that you aren't passionate about you aren't going to enjoy the training. That advice had stuck with me. I loved it and I had come so far with it, and invested so much time. It had changed my life; I had so many great opportunities come from just being in the sport. I met some amazing people: the prime minister at the time, Prince Harry, and I went to many big events, did public speaking and met sponsors. My life had changed and I wanted to continue on in that sport.

Once Rio was approaching I needed a change - a change in environment and a change of coach - so I moved to Melbourne. That was at the end of 2015/ start of 2016 and I continued working, training and racing all over the world, with several different guides and a new coach. I just really enjoyed my time in Melbourne: I learnt a lot more about life and had relationships. But I was also still learning more about my disability and the disability world. When I got into triathlon, over the years, I found my voice and decided that I had a lot to share and I felt like I had a lot to say. I felt that I could help people through talking about all my previous life experiences and the process I'd been through to accept my disability. To state that I had a disability and to be proud of it, and that I was part of a family. I was part of the Paralympic movement. I was a part of things that were bigger than me which I didn't have before; I had found identity and purpose through sport.

In 2018 I won a really big race over in Edmonton, Canada. It was at that time the medal events that were going to be given out in triathlon in Tokyo were announced, and we had six categories of disability at that stage, and were given 4 medal events. Even though we had four medal events we still had two categories that were missing out, but this time I was extremely fortunate to be in one of those medal events (or disability categories that had a medal event) in Tokyo, so that changed everything again.

I was being funded again by my national sporting federation; being supported in every way possible to be the best athlete I could be and to really reach my potential. I had to move again, to an elite high performance training environment, as if I wanted to reach my potential, I needed to be coached by a top level coach and there weren't any available where I was. I ended up moving to a regional town called Wollongong, which is basically halfway between Nowra and Sydney where I grew up. It's on the coast of New South Wales and in a beautiful part of the world. It was really good for me to move back there. I had spent so many years away from all my family and friends, including my siblings who were living in Sydney. To live right in-between all of that was a really big thing for me. Also to be training in a really great environment, have access to all the things I needed to train at my best, and to have access to a really good coach.

I've been in Wollongong now for 18 months and I'm getting really good results. At the time of writing this, I'm ranked number 3 in the world and I've all but secured a spot in the Tokyo Paralympics. In our sport, to qualify for the Games, there is a twelve month qualifying window which started in July 2019. It was supposed to go to July 2020, before the

Games were postponed. In that window your three best results are counted towards qualifying, and if your three best results (or your ranking points) mean that you qualify within the top ten you will get a spot within the Paralympic Games.

I've already got my three races done at the time of writing and I'm currently ranked third in the qualifying period. Although qualifying hasn't finished yet, and the current Covid-19 crisis means there is a big set back, as we have to wait until it is safe for everyone to travel again around the world, and travel to all the races and restart the qualification period again, we know that all the races are already completed in that window count. So, no matter what happens, I know that I have done everything I needed to and I have pretty well qualified.

When I get the plane ticket that says you're going to Tokyo I'll get excited, but I still need to wait until that time for that. I am so close now. If Tokyo was this year, it would have been an 8 year journey to get here.

One extra year to the Games, although it is disappointing, means the goal posts have just been shifted - it doesn't mean the Games have been taken away. For me, I have already taken a setback for Rio 2016, so I've already taken another four years to get to this point; it's already been eight years, so for me, another year, I feel fine with that. It gives me another year to train and get even better than I would have been in August 2020 when the games would have been. I take the positives out of it. I'm going to continue living here in Wollongong and keep training and staying focused on being the best athlete I can be.

That takes me right up to where I am now. Some of the lessons I have learnt. Having a disability has made me more resilient despite all the things I've already spoken about before I accepted my disability; the mental health issues, going through that whole process of losing my identity and purpose have contributed to how I feel now. Having come out of that the other side, and having learnt from that, has made me a much stronger person and made me feel more empowered. I feel like I have a lot of courage and I feel more independent than I ever was before.

I have a lot to give back to the community. It isn't just about my sport; it is about what my story can do to help others. When I was younger, sport was the one thing that got me through life and that was the one thing that kept me healthy and focussed. I gave that up when I was about 18 years old, and it took me ten years to find my way back into sport. I feel like I have picked my life back up again from when I left it. Life has just come full circle, and sport was always the thing that was going to be the answer. I have graduated with a sports management degree. I'm working towards a career in the sports industry and sport has given me everything. I am giving back as much as I can to that community and to other communities too.

The one message I can give to people out there who are reading this is to find something you are passionate about. Life is hard whether you have a disability or not, and I think if you have something in your life, whatever it is, find something that makes you happy and something you can push yourself in. Something you can challenge yourself in, learn from, grow in and get better at, and essentially you'll become a better person because of.

I'm sure that those that have that will understand what I am saying and those that don't - maybe you haven't found your passion yet. When you do you'll know what I am talking about. It makes everything clearer and you have something to aim for.

Follow Jono's paralympic journey on social media:

Facebook: www.facebook.com/JonathanGoerlachAthlete/
Instagram: @jonathangoerlach

London, UK based Amanda developed a photographic sense in the darkness

Sometimes when we follow our joy, instead of thinking about what is logically possible, it leads to us trusting our intuition and honing our other senses more than we had previously. Amanda has discovered that following her joy of photography has led her to not only realising a smaller dream, but recognising that her biggest dream is now a possibility...

Photo description: Amanda Ramsay sitting on a chair on a patio, facing the camera wearing sunglasses.

My name is Amanda and I was registered as a visually impaired person when I was 22 years old.

My sight has always been pretty bad since I was little but, when I was 14, I went for a routine eye exam and was told my vision had got a lot worse. They couldn't really see a reason why but I was told then that I would never be able to drive and just got on with my life. At that time of my life, I discovered rock music and Green Day and that really helped a lot.

My parents and my family have been absolutely amazing throughout my life. I got through normal school, with my fantastic friends helping me to read the board and helping me copy notes and stuff. I always had a bit of a lazy eye, but in my teenage life it seemed to get a lot worse and that is when my mum first got in contact with Moorfields Eye Hospital, as she was worried there was something seriously wrong with my eyes.

That was probably when I was about 17 and since then I have been visiting Moorfields who have been so helpful. It has taken a while to get a diagnosis as my condition does not tick all the boxes of certain things, but I have been diagnosed with cone dysfunction because of having a condition called Bardet-Biedl Syndrome (BBS).

At 20, I had an operation to help me with my lazy eye and it seems to have helped a lot. That was my first operation in my life and I was really scared. At the time I was in the middle of my course at Herts University and, again, I managed to get through it by having great friends and a great social life. I absolutely loved being a student and will never forget the time I spent there and the people I met.

I managed to get through my degree at Uni, which I absolutely loved, but I had a friend who was really good at photography and I thought I would give it a go. When I finished my studies, I had to register with another optician and that was the first time anyone had ever said to me that I was a visually impaired person. The optician asked me to go through my GP to get referred back to Moorfields Eye hospital.

Since then, I have had a lot of tests and eye exams to determine what is actually wrong. They thought that I had a condition called Achromatopsia but I have been given the diagnosis of having cone dysfunction. It is so great to have a diagnosis as it has taken a long time to find this out, but I am so grateful to my parents and Moorfields Eye Hospital for all their help with this.

The first camera that I bought was a tiny little point and shoot camera that was pink and I loved it! I took it on my holidays and my outings and just played around with it really. That started my love for taking photos. The first time I knew I really wanted to try and succeed as a photographer was in 2011. I entered a photo into the Herts Open Arts Exhibition and won the under 30's art prize for my shot of a Heron. It gave me the confidence and drive to really want to exhibit my photos.

After that, I saved up and bought my first proper camera. It wasn't a DLSR but it was a bridge camera and it was a lot more technical and a lot better than my little pink one! I also went to college to learn the basics of photography, and went out as much as possible taking photos of things. As you can imagine, I can't really see too much of the subject that I am taking, especially if I am outdoors in the sunshine, but I take loads of shots and then come home and have a look on my monitor to see if I have any good ones. My camera is also pretty noisy, so I know when it has taken a shot which helps a lot.

One of my traits, which I am sure is just as bad as good sometimes, is that I am a very stubborn person and I wanted to prove that, despite my bad eyesight, I could do anything that I wanted with my life. I have never given up, despite having to work really hard for what I want, even if people think it is a bit mad!

I was registered as a visually impaired person as I really cannot deal with bright light and have really bad photophobia. I am really lucky as Moorfields Eye hospital managed to find me some really dark tinted contact lenses so I can deal with the glare inside and I have to wear category 4 sunglasses outside to deal with the sunshine. I would not be able to deal with the outside world otherwise.

I'm also really fortunate to have enough sight to get on with what I want to do in my life, and that I was born into a world where there is a lot of technology to help when I need it!

I know it sounds completely bizarre to a lot of people that I am a partially sighted person and a photographer at the same time! It is what I truly love doing. I believe I understand the camera quite a bit because I can relate to it like my eyes. For example, I can understand exposure because it is a bit like my eyesight not dealing with bright light: photography is all about understanding lighting and how it affects an image.

As I am a member of my local arts group, I have been able to exhibit my photos in my local town and have sold a few. It gives me such happiness to know that someone loved a photo that I have taken so much that they have bought it. In 2020, the arts group asked me to have my own gallery of work up and I was so excited to have my first proper gallery. Unfortunately, due to the Coronavirus, it has been postponed as the gallery is shut. I hope to have many more exhibits in the future.

I have my sad days, where I really doubt myself and wonder why I am trying to achieve this, but it makes me even more determined to prove all the naysayers wrong. One day I want to have my own gallery in London, with all my work hanging up and then I can say that I finally made it!

My thanks go out to all my friends and family for always helping me out with my journey. Without them, I just wouldn't have been able to achieve what I have so far.

Thanks so much for reading my story. If you would like to have a look at my photography, I have my photos up online at www.flickr.com/mandyclarkie

Follow Amanda on social media:

Instagram: @mandytographer
Photography website: www.flickr.com/mandyclarkie

Dave, 'The Blind Poet' from Manchester, UK, is proud that his tunnel of darkness has inspired him to provide the light of hope to others all over the world

Sometimes, it's going through our darkest times that directs us towards our inner light, which we can then use to shine bright and lead the way for others out of their own darkness. This is exactly the journey Dave found himself travelling...

Photo description: Dave Steele wearing a three piece suit, facing the camera holding a cane.

Dave Steele is an award-winning poet, author, public speaker, singer, and advocate for the blind. Diagnosed with Retinitis Pigmentosa (RP) in 2014, this genetic eye condition left Dave "severely sight impaired." Together with his wife, Amy, the family grappled with the difficult diagnosis, as RP quickly left Dave an unemployed father of four.

Feeling the stressors of financial debt and the loss of his independence, Dave turned to social media for support with his RP journey. He was also struck by the numerous misconceptions and stories of injustice being experienced by so many blind/visually impaired people all over the world. When a member in one of these online groups learned of Dave's singing background, they invited him to perform at a meeting for those living with RP and Usher Syndrome. The experience inspired Dave's idea for his "Stand By Me RP" song. Using the classic song by Ben E. King, Dave altered the lyrics to relate to how he felt losing his own sight to Retinitis Pigmentosa. In December 2014, Dave sought permission from the band Elbow to alter the lyrics of their song "One Day Like This". With the band's blessing, Dave performed his version of the song at Joanne Milne's "Breaking the Silence" book launch.

Don't worry about tomorrow

For sight you're yet to lose

Don't waste the opportunity

to live the life you choose

Though there are limitations

and challenges each day

You'll overcome each obstacle each thing put in your way

I know some days are harder

than other ones to face

You're not alone

don't stay at home

This world is still your place

Today will be amazing

Just grab your cane and go

Use every tear and anxious fear to push you on and grow

It's up to you to show them

these misconceptions wrong

Just because we are disabled doesn't mean that we're not strong

Just because you say you're blind

it doesn't mean that you can't see

Just because I've got anxiety doesn't mean that I'm not me

Just because I'm smiling

doesn't mean I don't get sad

Just because I cry sometimes doesn't mean this life's so bad

Just because I talk to you doesn't mean that I'm not quiet

Just because I struggle

doesn't mean that I won't try it

Just because the sights I love

I see through tunnelled view

Just because I worry that my kids are 1 in 2

Just because I wish that doctors soon will find a cure

Just because tomorrow is a future still unsure

Just because the last of 5 degrees

will soon be gone

Just because you doubted me

I'll always carry on

Just because I wish sometimes that I was how I was

Just because I'll love my life with sight loss

just because

#TheBlindPoet

Dave created his own "Stand By Me RP" Facebook page in 2015. Since its conception, the page has become one of the largest social media RP groups in the world. As his eyesight continued to decline, the words did not stop flowing. Dave began writing two to three poems per day about his struggles and experiences. Part creative genius, part therapy, Dave's writing became a catalyst for helping others and himself through RP.

His first book, *Stand By Me RP Volume I*, was released in February 2016. That same day, he received the call that he had been matched with a guide dog. During its first week, *Stand By Me RP Volume I*, went on to become the #1 poetic release in both America and Australia.

In March of 2016, Dave left his family for 10 days to be trained with his guide dog, Christopher, a yellow Labrador retriever. He released his second book, *Stand By Me RP Volume II*, in February 2017. It became the #1 poetry release in Europe within its first day. In February 2018, Dave's third book, *Stand By Me RP Volume III* was released, completing his trilogy.

Dave has been featured in a short film by Cambridge University called *Blindsighted*. He has also appeared on a special called *the Blind Poet* for RNIB radio, BBC TV, ITV and That's Manchester TV news.

His advocacy work continues to be recognized both locally and internationally. In 2018, Dave was honored by Henshaws with the "Impact Award" and was the recipient of the Pride of Bury "Community Hero Award". He currently serves as a local ambassador for Henshaws and as a global ambassador for the American company, Two Blind Brothers.

In November 2019, Dave landed in the USA to kick off his first American Book Tour, sponsored by Low Vision Specialists of Maryland & Virginia and The Low Vision Shop. The three week tour included a wide variety of speaking engagements (keynote speeches, book readings/signings, meetings, and more) and visited major cities throughout the Northeast. Dave's presence uplifted the crowd throughout every step of the journey. Some of the book tour visits included the New York Public Library, Rhode Island College, Blind Industries and Services of Maryland (BISM), National Federation of The Blind Maryland

Conference, Maryland Department of Rehabilitation Services Conference, The Sight-Loss Support Group of Greater Baltimore, VisionCorps, and many more.

Dave's legion of followers greatly identifies with his poetic realism. With over 700 poems and songs dealing with the fears and struggles associated with sight loss, Dave' work is helping to diminish many of the misconceptions associated with blindness. His mission through his poetic verse is: "to help those who are being isolated by a condition that strips us of our independence, let them know that they aren't alone, and help educate loved ones on how we feel".

Follow Dave on his website and on social media:

Website: www.theblindpoet.net and www.theblindpoet. net/about-dave-steele/
Facebook: www.facebook.com/theblindpoet
Twitter: @BlindPoetRP
Instagram: @blindpoetrp

Canadian Christopher never says never to seeing new possibilities on his horizon

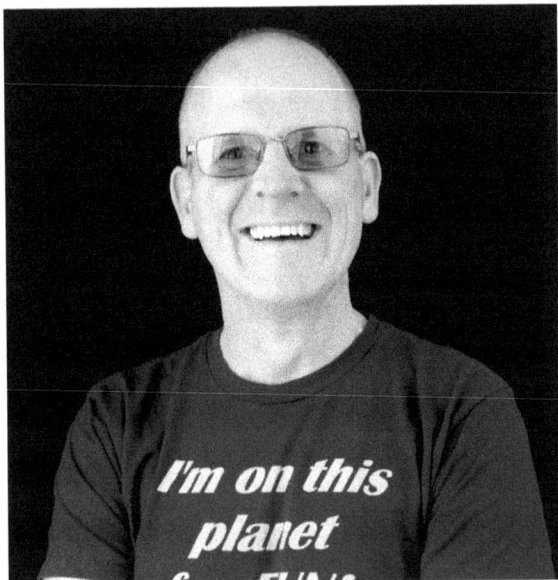

Life can be all about perception. After a loss, we can choose to focus only on that loss moving forwards or, like Christopher, learn to use our story for our purpose and set new goals to accomplish. Christopher knows that this can make life not only meaningful, but even fun!

Photo description: Christopher Warner facing the camera smiling, wearing a t-shirt with the slogan on "I'm on this planet for fun".

My name is Christopher Warner and I live in Calgary, Alberta, Canada. I was born with a condition called hydrocephalus, or water on the brain. To relieve the pressure from the fluid build up around my brain, a shunt consisting of two catheters and a small back-flow reservoir valve was installed in my body when I was three-months old. The shunt drains fluid from the ventricles of my brain to another part of my body where it can be better absorbed.

Despite having to go in for annual revisions to the shunt as I grew, I had a pretty normal childhood. I went to regular public schools, got good grades, and participated in everything my classmates did, with the exception of some physical education classes. There was always a risk of damage to the shunt, so any activity where the teachers believed I might get hurt, I had to either sit out or wear a hockey helmet, and I was never allowed to play any contact sports.

The shunt revisions stopped at age 10 because the surgeon told me he put in some extra catheter for me to "grow into", as he put it. His plan worked really well for the next 21 years.

Fast forward to 2005: I was living in Toronto, Ontario, Canada, had been married for nine years, and had a great job working in my chosen career at a television station. One day in October of that year, I wasn't feeling well and needed to be taken to hospital. I had emergency surgery to replace my shunt because it had failed. In fact, there were two surgeries within a 24-hour period because the first one didn't work.

When I woke up from that second surgery, all I could see was light and shadow.

Upon investigation, it was discovered I had experienced a stroke sometime between the two surgeries. The part of my brain that processes eyesight had been starved for blood due to the pressure put on it by the fluid around my brain. My eyes were fine, but my brain was not processing the signals from my eyes. The neurosurgeon told me I would likely recover some of my sight, but he couldn't tell me how much. He said to give it a year and see what happened.

Seven months later, on a return visit to the neurosurgeon, he said I had likely recovered as much as I was going to, a sentiment that was echoed by the neuro-ophthalmologist at the hospital. By that point, I had recovered some sight, but was still considered legally blind.

In the two to three years that followed the stroke, I went through all five stages of grief, denial, anger, bargaining, depression, and acceptance while I grieved the person I had been before my sight loss. Family and friends, along with the doctors and staff from CNIB, the Canadian National Institute for the Blind, were very helpful in my recovery. I was provided with helpful tools and assistance in regaining my abilities and self confidence.

In the time after the stroke, while I was recovering at home, my wife suggested I keep a journal of my experiences, thoughts and feelings while I recovered. Some friends and family members said they would like to read the journal some day, which inspired me to write my first book, a memoir called 'Life's not Over, It Just Looks Different.'

I self-published the book, meaning I was in charge of everything from hiring someone to edit it, to marketing and promoting it. Since its release in 2016, the book has sold in five countries, including Canada, the United States, and the United Kingdom. The book was released in print and e-book, which is my preferred way to read now, because my smart phone reads the book to me.

I thought the memoir would be my one and only book release, but I really liked the process of writing, editing, and everything involved in the marketing and promoting of it, so I decided that if another book idea came along, I would love to do it again.

In 2018, I was doing a presentation on behalf of CNIB for a class of Grade one students and, during the presentation, I was asked about guide dogs. Another child raised her hand and asked why there aren't any guide cats, and we had some fun talking about the behaviour of cats and why they would not make a good guide.

Back at the CNIB office, I was talking to a colleague about the presentation and the conversation about guide cats. He thought it was funny and asked if I had ever thought of writing a children's book. That gave me an idea and I set to work thinking of other animals a person would have misadventures with if they were used as guides.

With the help of a friend, who is a very talented artist, we created 'Tommy Wants a Guide Dog', the story of a young boy with sight loss and a big imagination. Since its release, in April 2020, it has sold in three countries.

Prior to losing my sight, I had adopted the philosophy that I am on this planet for fun, and although my sight loss definitely tested that thinking, it did not break me. Over the past 15 years I have travelled more places, met amazing people, and accomplished things I had never imagined when I was fully sighted.

These days, I'm still doing presentations on behalf of CNIB, as well as speaking about my books. There are many ideas on the go in my computer, so I don't know what my next book will be about or when it will be released, but I've learned to never say never and just keep having fun.

Follow Christopher on social media:

Instagram: @lifesnotover_ca and @nakokitabooks
Book websites: www.lifesnotover.ca and
www.nakokitabooks.com

Nigel from Nottingham, UK, defied death to live his wildest dreams with eye sight loss

Sometimes it can be the very thing that sent us down a path of seeming destruction that sets us back on our path of purpose. Nigel is now #EyeInspiring others due to reclaiming his passions...

Photo description: Nigel Limb sat on a train looking out of the window.

Hello, my name is Nigel and I'm 55 years old.

8 months after my 50th birthday I was participating in a lifelong passion of mine, motorbike speedway, when I was involved in a freak accident where I suffered major brain damage.

When I finally woke out of my coma it was clear that I had some sight loss and was diagnosed with purchase retinopathy. It took quite a long time for me to realise the impact of my eyesight loss; several weeks after I came out of my coma in fact, because my brain was still swollen at that time. It really hit home when my wife sadly had a mental breakdown, got sectioned and put into a mental institution. I then started realising the impact of my eyesight loss, which had all happened, obviously, in the blink of an eye.

Until then I'd had my own business for 27 years; I was a successful business person and I had many passions and dreams, and it was quite clear to me that my eyesight loss was going to stop all of these in one hammer-blow. So that realisation then sent me into a spiral of mental distress. I'd realised that I'd lost my wife to the mental institution, and I'd lost my business.

I'd felt as though I'd lost the chance to live my passions again forever, so I then started to feel suicidal, which was never me, but at the time I felt that that was the only way out. Thankfully, I didn't follow through with it and I'm now here, 5 years later.

Ironically, my success in life and passions was the Achilles heel that actually sent me on a downhill spiral. Ironically, it was also my success, my passions and my desire for life, that actually brought me back, because I decided that I would like to regain my passions, albeit in a different manner. That drove me to chip away, day by day, at everything that I now do, which includes being a motivational speaker.

I've ridden motorbikes since that decision; I do various challenges on motorbikes and in cars. I've ridden a speedway bike, I've ridden a hot-rod, and I've been away with the wall of death.

One of my passions before my accident, my eyesight loss, was photography. I was a semi-professional photographer a number of years ago. I've revisited photography and I had a successful photographic exhibition last year. That first exhibition was called 'Life on Mars' and included pictures to depict my life since my accident with my vision loss.

I was due to have one again this year but the Coronavirus pandemic stopped that, so I'm aiming now for next year, and the next exhibition I'm going to have will be based on my time away with the wall of death attraction.

Follow Nigel on social media:

Facebook: www.facebook.com/nigel.limb.1
Instagram: @blindblokeracing

Iranian Atiyeh's sudden darkness helped to shine a light on her true path in life

Atiyeh Shahsavari Fard's story shows that sometimes it takes being thrown into complete darkness to guide us away from what we feel we should be doing, in order to find the life path on which we belong; then we need to believe, believe, believe we CAN achieve. Atiyeh is living proof of the power of this belief...

Photo description: Atiyeh Shahsavari Fard stood outside facing the camera, with greenery behind her, holding to the side of her hat.

Hello, I am Atiyeh Shahsavari Fard and I was born in 1996. I am an Iranian and I have always lived here but I have many experiences of living in different cities such as Rasht, Shiraz, Tehran and Karaj - because of my father's job we have moved a lot. It was a very good opportunity for me to become a social child and to communicate with people easily, as I always had to find new friends in new places during those days.

I would really like to be a doctor. I was often dreaming about doing brain surgery. I was very good at my school courses, so everyone was certain that I would be able to study medicine, but as I reached the age of 13 suddenly everything changed. It all began with a simple headache one day when I was at school. I felt a very drastic headache so I asked my mom to take me home and she did. My parents observed that I was not getting better so they took me to hospital to be examined by a specialist. They did some scans of my brain and said it was not a serious problem but that it would be better to be in hospital for the next 24 hours.

The next day, as I opened my eyes, I found everywhere completely dark. My parents called the doctor, and the early diagnosis from the medical team was MS and they claimed that I will gain my eyesight very soon again, but it never happened. We were all shocked and nobody knew what was happening, and my pain was growing every day. So my family decided to take me to another hospital, when the new examinations showed that I was suffering from high pressure of the brain and the primary diagnosis was incorrect. They also added that the previous medical team had lost the "golden period of time" to save my eyesight and my optic nerves had been destroyed under the pressure. It was a real calamity for me and my family, I was so confused at that time, I had no idea of how a blind person's life could be.

But I decided to return to school, after just 2 months. I started to study in my previous school with my other friends, because I didn't even know that there were special schools for blind people. I didn't have any audio books, so my mother read all the books to me and I had to try to memorise them all. Despite all these problems I passed my exams by a grade. The only issue which was bothering me was that I couldn't study medicine anymore, and they told me that I must study theoretical sciences. USING Jaws I passed my ICDL courses of computer successfully and I received my international certificate of ICDL - according to this, as I finished my high school, I was accepted in the university of Tehran, the best and greatest university in Iran. It was like a dream for me, because even normal students were not able to enter this university easily, and I decided to study political science.

During my years of bachelor study, I was always in the 3 top students, so I decided not to concentrate on just one aspect, I started music - I took some courses in piano and guitar. I also learnt swimming and chess. I completed my English in the first year of university and I took my TTC certificate from which I was allowed to teach English. So then I started to learn French and German too. At the same time I met a multi-lingual professor who encouraged me to learn more languages as he saw I could learn so fast, so I added Spanish and Italian to my plan too as I finished my bachelor degree.

I was chosen by best ranking for master studies as I was really interested in European culture. I chose regional studies of Europe. I am also getting ready for my PHD and, as I need a perfect CV for this, I am going to translate a book about EU security policy into Persian. I am working on two articles related to my field and I have started some new languages such as Russian Arabic and Hindi. Of course not very seriously yet, but I have a plan to know 10 languages by the next 5 years and now I have stopped my music courses because I am so busy with university affairs! Though I hope I will be able to continue music after my PHD entrance exam.

Even though sight loss was a real shock for me and changed my way of life, it showed me many new ways. I learned so many new things that I could never imagine. I believed in myself after I did so much work that even my able-sighted friends were not able to do. I must mention that my parents have played a very important role during all these years - they never let me feel I have something less than others and supported me in all my hardships. Now

I have many plans for my future, and I am trying to make myself completely qualified for them.

I would like to become a professor in my university and I also dream about working in the UN as I have concentrated on the peace topic - I am sure that I can do it. I never gave up during my worst times and I will never do so. I would also really like to communicate with people from different places to know more about their cultures and lifestyles.

I have always been around sighted people and I have worked and learnt beside sighted people - I do not have many visually impaired friends. So my next goal is to find some new friends with vision impairment to learn about their experiences and share my experiences with them. Getting to know Eye Inspire was a great opportunity for me to do so.

Follow Atiyeh's ongoing progress on;

Instagram: @atiyeh.shahsavari

Declan from New York, USA is proud that he achieved what he set his sights on, and urges that you can too!

Declan Ryan doesn't give up easily. Sometimes being told we can't do something makes us even more determined, and Declan is no stranger to determination. Once told he wouldn't even be able to graduate from senior school due to his visual disability, Declan is now racing towards new goals he'd never dreamed possible. As he says: 'if you set your mind to something, then any obstacle can be overcome'...

Photo description: Declan Ryan crouched down on one knee facing the camera with his black assistance dog.

I was born with LCA (Leber's Congenital Amaurosis). Despite being told I would be totally blind by the age of 10, and also being misdiagnosed, I had a normal childhood and education up until it came time for high school. Both the school's principal and my mother thought it would be a good idea if I attended a public high school instead of a private school, so I would get the proper vision services I was entitled to through New York State Commission for the Blind. Little did we know that it would be the beginning of an extensive battle with New York lawmakers and Board of Education officials. I was told to choose 12 schools that I wanted to attend and, based on that list, I would be placed in one of them. When the decision day came, I was only given one out of the 12 options I chose, and it just so happened to be the last choice on the list.

For lack of a better term, the school was not ideal for someone with a visual impairment, or any other handicap for that matter. Upon advice of school officials, I went anyway just to give it a test run during a normal school day. It was made clear that within an hour of me being there it was not going to be a safe fit for a blind student. After talking with that high school's administration, they informed me that I should take my concerns, along with their recommendations, to the New York department of education and have them assign me to one of the other schools I had chosen that would be best at accommodating for someone who was visually impaired. This would only lead to a lengthy drawn out battle that involved lawyers and confronting the school's chancellor and former mayor of New York face to face.

Once again, I went around to schools I felt best fit me and all of them pretty much turned a deaf ear to a blind child. One of which even went as far as to tell me directly they were not equipped to handle someone who is handicapped whilst a student in a wheelchair passed by in front of me. It was at that point that home school became the only viable option for my freshman year of high school.

By some miracle, one day my mother ran into the mom of a former classmate of mine and they started discussing my issue. It was only then my former classmate's mom recommended the school that her child was in. Based on her recommendation we figured it couldn't hurt for me to interview at that school. The next morning, I walked in and was greeted by the high school principal who asked me one simple question, what do I want out of my high school career? To which I replied I only want a chance at a fair education. At that moment the principal said, OK fine, you start first thing tomorrow and we will assist you with whatever services you need. At that time, it became clear the nightmare of dealing with New York politicians and the board of education would finally come to an end. Dealing with lawyers and politicians at an early age is never easy but it prepared me for life's adventures that lay ahead.

The remainder of my high school education was mostly uneventful up until it came time for the dreaded SAT in my senior year. Like some students, I didn't want to take the test and had to deal with teachers and guidance counsellors wanting to know why I did not want to go to college. Every time I was asked the question I would always respond with: college is not for me, I want to pursue my dream of becoming a New York City firefighter. This is a dream of mine that I still hold to this day. Despite not wanting to take the SAT exam, I listened to the advice of my mom and took it anyway just as a fallback. Upon graduating high school, which was something those in the New York Department of Education thought I could never do, I ended up attending college after all since the exam to become a firefighter was not being given yet. Needless to say, I still found a way to pursue firefighting by getting my associate's degree in fire science. Most would think that a blind person cannot become a firefighter and to a certain extent they are correct. However, back in 2018, my dream became partial reality when the exam finally opened and I passed! That's correct - I once again did something most thought could not be accomplished; I successfully passed the written exam to become a New York City firefighter. Whilst that would be the furthest I could pursue my dream for now, the fact still remains that I graduated college with the knowledge of firefighting and passed the exam to become one of New York's bravest.

Some would say that when one door closes another one opens. I like to think this is true with my dream of becoming a firefighter to what has now become my running career. I first got into running back in 2009, while training to run a 5K race put on by the Tunnel to Towers foundation. Ironically enough, this race and its foundation were created in honour of a fallen New York City firefighter. Once again, society would think that someone who is visually impaired, or blind, can't participate in mainstream running events, but anything is possible if you put your mind to it and learn to adapt and overcome.

When I first started training, I would run in New York's iconic Central Park, or at a local soccer field on days when weather was not favourable for recreational teams or Little League. Yes, my vision was getting worse, but I was still able to see someone in front of me and detect an obstacle that might be in the way. When it came time to actually run the 5K race my sister reluctantly volunteered - she is not a runner! However, running alongside me the entire way, we finished the 3.1 mile race with a time of just over 40 minutes. Since then it has become an annual tradition that we run this race every year and, in doing so, it has led me to want to push my body further and run longer distances.

So, what better way to push yourself than get the idea that one day you can run the New York marathon, which is 26.2 miles. Not being crazy like myself, my sister did not want to partake in this adventure, so it was up to me to figure out a way to make this happen. For a couple of years, the idea of running New York's marathon was just a bucket list item, until October

2018. After graduating college and not working full-time, sitting around got boring really quick and getting out and being active running seemed like a good idea. After making posts on social media to see if anyone wanted to run with a blind guy, I was put in contact with Achilles International. This organization partners able-body athletes with those who have disabilities and want to get back into mainstream sports. It just so happened that one of the volunteers to answer my posting was training another visually impaired runner to take part in the New York marathon. They offered to have me come run with them to see if it was something I was interested in doing.

On our first training run I was lucky to make it 4 miles without having to stop and take a break. On that training run in October the trainer asked me what I wanted to do in terms of running races. I answered one day I would like to run the New York marathon, to which he replied, OK you will run it next year in 2019 with me. Even with only being able to make it 4 miles, the fact somebody was willing to train me to run 26.2 miles shows us all the kindness that people have towards those with disabilities, despite the negativity we can face at times.

I often get asked the question, how do you run a race if you cannot see? The answer is simple: the visually impaired athlete and a sighted guide hold onto a tether and simply go running. It is up to both the athlete and guide to be aware of what is going on at all times. The guide has to make sure they are giving the correct signals to the blind athlete as to avoid injury, and it is up to the athlete to pay attention to every verbal and felt sense signal given through the tether, to make sure there are no accidents. Having to trust someone with your safety whilst running is scary to some at times and accidents can happen. I've had my fair share of bumps and bruises and would be able to write my own book on them but, the main thing is, if you have fun doing something it's not about how hard you fall but how you get back up and go again.

The reality of participating in one of the world's largest races did not sink in fully until I received the registration confirmation. In January 2019 it was time to put training as a priority; running 4 miles quickly turned into a 6-mile training run and, thanks to my trainer, members of his family, and other volunteers with Achilles International, 6 miles rapidly became running a 10 and 15 K. By the end of the summer in 2019 I had completed my longest race to date of 18 miles in Central Park. Three weeks later it was time for the marathon; Super Bowl Sunday for those in the running community, if you will. Time to put a year's worth of training and exercise to the test. My guide, another volunteer and I got to the start line and before the smoke from the Start cannon cleared, we were off to the finish line.

Being born and raised in New York, you don't realize just how long the city can be until you are running through the streets of it. My trainer reiterated the three promises he made back when we were training:

you will not be the last person to cross the finish line, you will not be the first person to cross the finish line, but you will cross it safely and in one piece. Slightly over six hours later he was correct - we had finished my first ever, full-length marathon.

My next adventure is going to be running the New York 60K, which is a nearly 40 mile race, and just like training for the marathon, and achieving a proper high school education, and passing the firefighter exam, I'm ready and willing to meet the challenges that come with it.

Despite what others may tell you, anything is definitely possible if you put your mind to it: remember, you will just have to adapt and overcome. If I can do it then so can you!!

Follow Declan's progress on social media:

Facebook: www.facebook.com/declan.ryan.73
Instagram: @NYNJrunner556

Kai from Georgia, USA, is proud that he has learned to define himself, rather than allowing his sight loss to define him

Kai Owens is determined to be the best version of himself he can possibly be; being classed as legally blind doesn't stop him setting his sights on dreams that many sighted people don't even hold. What an inspiration he is at only 17! Hear what Kai gets up to below ...

Photo description: Kai Owens, facing the camera holding two fingers up as a peace sign, wearing a t-shirt with the slogan "I can't count your fingers" and the equivalent braille interpretation.

I am a legally blind action sports enthusiast. I surf, skate, and I am sponsored for skim-boarding. I am also a musician; I play rock and blues locally, but spend most of my time practicing extreme metal. I have also had the highest GPA in my grade for six of the past seven years (one year of those six was a tie). I refuse to let anything stand in the way of my goals and dreams. I believe that anyone can accomplish anything if they are willing to put in the time and work.

I started losing my vision in 4th grade at the age of 10. My parents knew something was wrong because I started having super bad anxiety for the first time ever, and we began the trips to doctors trying to figure out why. My mom then realized that it was something to do with my vision when I was writing on a paper and kept starting in the middle of the page. So we went to an eye doctor and they could not fix my vision with glasses, so they sent us on the journey to several other eye doctors where I was eventually diagnosed with Retinitis Pigmentosa. But it was seemingly unusual. And now, I am back to doctors once more trying to figure out what it is exactly. I am now 17 and have very little central vision except for a small spot in the center of each eye, and I still have some of my peripheral vision.

I grew up doing board sports from as young as 3 years old. My older brother liked skateboarding, so I learned quickly. By age 5, I was dropping in on five foot quarter pipes and trying to shred. I also began skim-boarding at around age 4 on our occasional beach trips. Jumping forward several years, I attended a skim-boarding camp on my home beach with World Champion, Austin Keen. He was impressed and very supportive and ended up helping me get sponsored by the company that he rides for, Exile Skimboards. I began attending competitions which ended in varying levels of success but definitely surprised the audience when they were told I am legally blind. In the middle of all of this, I learned to surf, wakeboard, longboard and, recently, I learned to snowboard. I met many challenges in these sports but none were impassible; I always found ways around my obstacles. In skateboarding, I usually skate with my cane, and just make sure I know the area and spot I am skating. In skim-boarding, I learn how the waves break at whatever beach I am at and find the placement and timing of the waves with my remaining sight, but if the glare is strange on the water I can have a friend call out when to go for a wave. In snowboarding, I have a guide wearing a vest calling out turns while riding in front of me, so I can follow his path, and we will sometimes go over the basic route of the run before starting down the slope and stop when I need more information on the slope.

I began my journey in music at age 12 on a drum-set. Now, I have been playing for nearly seven years and have played many gigs and learned tons of songs. I am especially interested in progressive metal and technical deathcore, where the drumming is insane. From odd time signatures to nested tuplets and metric modulation, I am fascinated with advanced rhythmic concepts. Out of this love for drumming came an interest in all music theory and all types of music. I now plan to attend college for music theory and composition, with plans to be a performer and possibly a professor.

In school, I have also had my challenges and successes. I had to learn braille and assistive technology to be able to access material for honors and AP classes, and braille has been one of the most important things I have ever learned. I also use a cane for all my travel and have been approved for a guide dog from Guiding Eyes and am awaiting a match. Learning the hard things and putting in the extra work is what I had to do to be successful. As someone with a visual impairment, there are no shortcuts; it is all just grinding out the work that needs to be done and learning the necessary skills.

My mentor, Joe Strechay, taught me that it's important to put in the work and tell people who I am. Nothing is easy if it is worthwhile. Learning and perfecting a skill takes time and no matter what your physical abilities are that stands true. So along with this ideology, I had to accept my vision loss quickly and fully, because I had goals and refused to be left in the dust. I am legally blind, and I would rather be the best visually impaired version of myself than be in denial, pretending like everything is okay while being a fake, unsuccessful person acting sighted. Refusing to accept your situation will never make it better, and if I hadn't accepted myself I would not have accomplished anything near what I have now. Being blind/VI is only one part of a person; do not let it define you - define yourself.

Follow Kai on social media:

Facebook: www.facebook.com/navigatingblindness
Instagram: @kai.owens and @navigatingblindness
Website: www.navigatingblindness.com

Alice from London, UK, is proud that she has been able to succeed as a VIP (Visually Impaired Person)

Alice now encourages others with a sight impairment to utilise the things that helped her succeed in realising her dreams: not being afraid to ask for support, finding a community which can act as your rock, and practicing positive self-talk. Now, Alice sings her own song...

My name is Alice Cadman and I have a rare eye condition called Stargardt's Disease. I am a professional singer and run a primary school music organisation, Sing Education.

I grew up with completely 'normal' vision, although, when I look back, there were hints at some strange things going on with my vision - always wanting the light on as a child, even on a bright summer's day. I attended regular eye tests, I was an avid reader, I could sight-read music fluently as a singer, oboist and pianist, and I learnt to drive. It wasn't until I was aged twenty-two, and beginning my first year of a music degree at a conservatoire, that I started to notice changes in my vision. My friends had to jump around so that I could find them. I became a nervous driver – lanes suddenly seemed to disappear, and I once only noticed a parked lorry just in time.

I went for an optician's appointment, expecting to come out with a lovely pair of glasses. But the optician spotted something strange and gave me a referral. Fast forward a few months and I received a letter for an appointment at a genetic clinic. I was confused – no one in my family has a major problem with their eyes so I thought it must be a mistake!

At the appointment, they did some tests and diagnosed me with macular dystrophy. My memory of this appointment is vague; I wasn't prepared for it, I wasn't expecting them to tell me that something was seriously wrong with my sight. Had I caused it somehow? Aside from giving up driving straight away, I carried on living as I had before, with little knowledge of the condition and not yet ready to seek help. It was only as I started to tell friends and family about it, and as I began to discuss my needs at university, that I realised this might have quite an impact on my life.

I was soon introduced to a university tutor who supported students with extra learning needs. We got on well and, as it happened, she had a very similar eye condition. I know that meeting this tutor so early on in my sight loss journey had a hugely positive impact on the years that followed, and on how my sight loss impacted my life. Meeting her meant that I was prepared for what was to come. My new friend and tutor warned me that doctors might suggest I needed time out of university, or that I might be told I should not expect to work. She showed me that somebody could thrive in the working world, despite vision loss. She taught me that life with sight loss was likely to be a challenge, that it wasn't going to be an easy ride, that the world can be very unfair for people living with disabilities. But, alongside that, she taught me that if you're willing to work hard and to advocate for yourself and others, you could show the world that sight loss is not a barrier.

Eventually, aged twenty-four, I was diagnosed with Stargardt's Disease and was registered as 'sight impaired'. Stargardt's is a juvenile, inherited condition, meaning that it usually comes out in childhood or early adulthood and is passed on genetically. No one in my family had Stargardt's – or had ever heard of it! Stargardt's affects your central vision, which is 'where you look', but it also deals with fine detail, straight lines and colour. When I was first diagnosed, I had a small missing patch of vision in my left eye. I remember constantly closing one eye and then the other. What would I do when it showed up in both eyes? I wouldn't be able to cope then, surely? I shared this worry with another tutor at my music college who, with family experience of sight loss, encouraged me not to live in fear, thinking every day – 'will it be worse tomorrow?'

University was simultaneously a wonderful and challenging place to deal with the onset of sight loss. On one hand, I had amazing friends and tutors around me who supported and encouraged me. On the other hand, I had some difficult conversations with people who did not understand what was happening to me. I struggled to get some essential support I needed having not yet learnt the skills to fight for accessibility. I very quickly realised that if I was going to do well in my degree, I was going to have to work extra hard. I was going to have to exercise my right to complain when I wasn't given support and I was going to have to learn to be organised!

I led a full student life; studying, teaching singing, piano and classroom music, and working as a waiter at parties and bars. Towards the end of my degree, I founded Sing Education, with my (now) husband and a friend. By the time I graduated, my vision had deteriorated quite a bit, leaving me with a large blank patch in the middle of both eyes and flashing white and green lights over the top.

My Christian faith sustained me through this time and continues to be my rock. I had a loving church community around me who built me up, alongside the support of my husband, close friends and family. I believed that God would use my visual impairment to help others. This seemed like an unlikely dream at the time, however, I eventually reached a stage where Stargardt's was no longer a negative thing in my life. Being visually impaired was something I had come to like about myself. I found that opportunities related to sight loss started coming my way: I received some funding grants and met many wonderful people. I now teach singing to a young girl who is blind; I've been involved in a project with The Amber Trust to empower other music teachers to teach children who are blind or partially sighted; I've sung in The Queen's Gallery, Buckingham Palace at an art event for visually impaired people; I've led sight loss awareness school assemblies; and I run an Instagram account, @ life_as_a_vip, to raise awareness of visual impairment.

I find that life as a visually impaired person (a "VIP") is a balancing act between proving that I can overcome the challenges of sight loss and be positive and successful, while also showing people that there are an array of daily challenges, mainly because society is simply not set up for people with disabilities. I believe that with education and awareness the world can become a more welcoming place for those with sight loss.

I encourage you to speak positively to yourselves – there is power in words. I encourage you to learn to describe your needs with confidence. I know this can be hard, but it is so worthwhile and will last you a lifetime. I encourage you to find a community where you can listen to and learn from one another. I encourage you to embrace technology – it is going to be your best friend. I encourage you to accept support and to grasp good opportunities when they come your way.

Find out more about Alice and her projects on social media;

Instagram: @life_as_a_vip
Website: www.lifeasavip.com
Business website: www.singeducation.co.uk
Singing website: www.alicecadman.co.uk

British Jesse Dufton
#Emerged Proud at the top of his climbing blind challenge

Jesse proves that, with a 'can-do' attitude, perseverance and the belief that there is a solution to every problem, anything is achievable. With his sight deteriorating from a very young age, Jesse has found a way around the challenges that most sighted people wouldn't deem possible. Accepting and giving support to his team-mates, resulted in towering strength for Jesse...

Photo description: Jesse Dufton facing the camera and smiling, wearing a woolen hat.

June 4th 2019

As I sat on the stony beach listening to the waves and feeling the wind and rain hit my face, I reflected on how my Scottish weather luck had finally ended. Climbers like myself often fall in love with the wild highlands that offer us a world-class adventure playground, but the capricious nature of the weather is not so endearing. I had been riding on a string of good weather luck across my trips north. In Reiff, Arran and the Cairngorms the weather had been blessedly benevolent. It seemed unfortunate then that my luck had run out on the day of my most significant climb to date. I was about to attempt to climb the Old Man of Hoy, a jewel of British climbing which is highly prized.

I sat with members of the film crew and hoped the weather would improve. Climbing in the rain is miserable, difficult and dangerous and the drone which would film me climbing couldn't fly in high winds.

So why would my ascent be filmed? Probably because I'm an unusual climber. I carry a genetic mutation which has gradually robbed me of my sight. I lost the ability to read years ago and, when I climb, I can't see any of the hand or foot holds or the climbing safety equipment as I place it. This is particularly significant as I would be leading this climb. Climbers normally climb as a pair with one leader who climbs up first and places the safety equipment into naturally occurring cracks as they go, and a seconder who climbs afterwards and retrieves the equipment as they follow up. Leading is hugely more difficult than seconding. You must hold on longer in order to place the gear and because the rope goes down from you, the consequences of falling off are dramatic and serious. This leads to the extra psychological difficulty of controlling the inherent fear. Because of this the routes which climbers lead are usually the yardstick by which they measure themselves. A blind person leading a route which is considered serious by experienced, sighted climbers is somewhat unusual, to say the least!

So how did I find myself about to attempt something beyond the comprehension of most? I like to joke that I didn't have much choice about getting into climbing. My dad was part of a Mountain Rescue Team and took me climbing as soon as I could walk. I seconded my first route aged 2 and led my first route aged 11. The fact that I had been diagnosed as severely sight impaired aged 4 didn't seem to be an issue as far as my parents were concerned, and I am eternally grateful that they instilled a can-do attitude in me from an early age.

I was born with no peripheral vision and only about 20% of central vision. I could just about guess at letters on the third line of the optician's eye chart. This isn't a great baseline, but for me it was the highpoint of my sight.

Despite my failing sight, I did well academically and went on to study Chemistry at the University of Bath. People often ask how I managed this, given I could never see well enough to read the board and had to struggle with a magnifier to read textbooks. I think 2 things are key. First, I was brutal about focusing in on the important information and, second, I worked out mnemonics to help myself remember it. For me the act of writing notes on what the lecturer said helped me to remember, even though I couldn't necessarily read back what I'd written afterwards.

Needless to say, work in a chemistry laboratory for my degree was "interesting", but the unenviable title of "Mr Smashy Smashy" went to someone else - my housemate, not me. This I regarded as a win! As soon as I could, I swapped lab work for Computational Chemistry, where I used computer models to simulate reactions or materials.

To my surprise this led to me being offered a Ph.D. position studying materials for photovoltaic solar cells. My sight had been gradually deteriorating throughout my university years, but in the first year of my Ph.D., the deterioration rate dramatically increased. I began to rely on text-to-speech software as magnification ceased to be sufficient for me to read conventionally. I often joke that I've written a doctoral thesis, but I've never read it.

My clean energy related Ph.D. allowed me to start working for a hydrogen fuel cell technology company. I completed a Graduate Training Scheme and was then sent to London to complete a Postgraduate

Certificate in Intellectual Property Law at Queen Mary's. This was a prerequisite for my current role in the Intellectual Property department, managing the firm's patents.

Perseverance and problem-solving were crucial in overcoming the challenges my eyesight presented in academia and at work. I was always determined to find a way, even if I didn't know what that was going to be at the outset. I guess it's these same qualities that have also enabled my climbing.

All through undergraduate, my Ph.D. and afterwards I had been climbing in my spare time. I'd made a group of good friends through the University Mountaineering Club and I'd been away climbing with them all over Europe. As my sight had deteriorated, my friends had started to help guide me. They started with small suggestions at first, then more frequent and more detailed instructions were needed as I had lost more and more of my sight.

For me parity of effort is really important. I don't want to be 'taken out climbing', I want to contribute as much as everyone else in the team. If my friends are helping me by directing, then I need to find a way to pull my weight. The best example of this metaphor is when I took it literally. We organised an expedition to Greenland and one of the best ways I could contribute to the team was to carry all the heavy equipment. I would exhaust myself so that my friends were fresher and more able to perform tasks I couldn't help with, like map reading and fixing the fiddly stove. I always volunteer to do the things I can, so I can accept help with the things which are hard because of my eyes, and everyone has still contributed equally.

So, I guess it's the combination of attitude, the years of experience and teamwork that had led me to the base of the Old Man of Hoy, to climb this 137m tall freestanding sandstone pillar rising straight up out of the ocean in the Orkney archipelago. It overhangs on every side and there is no easy way to the top. Fortunately, my misgivings about the weather were ill-founded. Whichever deity controlled the weather that day smiled upon me and in mid-afternoon I started the climb.

The crux is a section called "The Coffin" a small shoulder-width slot capped by an overhang. With no holds to pull on, I had to jam my hands into the crack above the roof and torque them, before contorting the rest of my body into a ball to attain the critical foothold. Meanwhile the roiling waves were crashing below me and seabirds were wheeling overhead. I like the fact that moments like this in climbing demand such total focus from you, forcing you to concentrate and try your hardest. I made it through this and the other subsequent tests which the climb presented.

While I am not one for displays of exuberance, those who know me well could see my satisfaction as I crested the top of the tower as the sun set beneath me.

Find out more at www.jessedufton.com

Follow Jesse on social media:

Facebook: www.facebook.com/JesseDuftonGBParaclimber
Twitter: @JesseDufton
Instagram: @JesseDufton

Canadian Cody is proud of his adventurous life, one he never believed would be possible

As Cody knows only too well, sometimes choosing what seems to be the hardest thing can lead to the best outcomes. We have to learn to love ourselves first and the rest will follow. Cody says; "If it wasn't for me starting to emerge proud of who I am, these things would have never happened." What a legend he is!

Photo description: Cody Campbell facing the camera smiling, with a mountain range in the background.

Hello everyone my name is Canadian Cody and I would like to share with you all the victories that I have had as a self-advocating DeafBlind backpacker, living and working abroad in New Zealand. I have Retinitis Pigmentosa Usher's Syndrome Type2.

I am severely hearing impaired, I wear hearing aids, and I am legally blind, but that has no longer stopped me from living a life that, two years ago, I would not have believed was possible. After going through a very hard time in my life I found myself in a position to leave everything behind and do something that I had never done before, travel solo.

Let me tell you this, choosing to travel was the best decision I ever made in my life. There are things that I have now done that I used to believe I would never be able to do in my lifetime. I am honestly blessed to have what I have, otherwise I probably wouldn't be sitting here writing to you about how rewarding it's been to find myself and to build up the courage and confidence to show the world that I am proud of who I am. I hope this story of the way I have been living my life will inspire you to start living yours.

My job, my driver's license, my girlfriend....I found myself hanging on tightly to these things I had established because I was afraid of losing them all. I felt that I had to stay forever doing the things I had been doing with the people I had been doing them with, because they were the only ones who knew of my vision loss. I felt that I would never be given a chance by people who didn't already know about me. I continued to hang on to the only life I thought I could ever have, I thought I could only do what I already knew how to, but even that was becoming a struggle. I was no longer a happy person, I was an angry one. I didn't have the confidence or self-esteem to make a positive change in my life. I never realized that those things I was afraid of losing were in fact the same things that were holding me back.

I finally had the mental breakdown my life needed after months and months of torturing myself and others with competition, jealousy, dangerous driving, drugs and alcohol, unrealistic expectations, violence, denial, and thoughts of suicide, among other things.

I got fired from my job of seven years and then decided to end my relationship with my girlfriend. She never accepted who I was becoming either. She never told her family what kind of person she was really with. We were together for six years. I couldn't learn to accept and love myself if she was still a part of my life. A huge weight had been lifted off of my shoulders and I was finally free and able to spread my wings. But I still had anger towards the fact that I had pretty much lived in the same houses as my mother for my whole life up until that point. So I spent the next two months planning my four month solo travel trip to New Zealand. Part of me leaving was to grow as a person, by challenging myself outside of my comfort zone and into the fear of the unknown.

Four, five, six months turned into one year going on two years and I'm still here in this amazing country today. The original four months were great but I was feeling like it wasn't enough of that challenge I was looking for, so I extended my stay. Doing this meant that I was going to have to start working and saving money. It's been a challenge to get work because of rejection for being legally blind. Many of the times I've had prolonged work experiences here is when I've hidden the fact that I was legally blind and managed to remain hidden for the duration of the work. Despite my challenges, I have worked as a fish freezer boat unloader, a chicken farm worker, a potato chip factory worker, a landscaper, a rubbish runner, a vineyard worker, a kiwi fruit thinner, and as a volunteer for an environmental disaster cleanup. It hasn't been easy. It's always been hard to do the jobs fast without seeming suspiciously slow.

I couldn't be upfront and honest with my employers about my disabilities or else I wouldn't have had those jobs. I've been judged for being slow and seeming lazy, I've been verbally abused, I've actually gotten into heated arguments over my visual impairment, and I've even been physically assaulted because of it. On the other hand, I've had people coming up to me telling me that they were sorry and feeling guilty that they ever judged me before knowing anything about me. I've had it where once I was able to advocate myself to the people I worked with, they actually started to help me keep up the pace so that the boss wouldn't notice me. I had that job for an extra two months because of that. I have been very empowered by my exposure to, and success in, different jobs that I used to believe I could never do because I am legally blind. I can honestly tell you that one of the main reasons I've managed to be here this long is because of how I've gone around with my cane and advocated for myself.

One of my goals when starting to travel was to become comfortable using my Identification Cane. Well, not only am I comfortable with it now, but I actually look forward to using it. I soon realized, once overcoming the self-consciousness associated with starting to use a cane, that it gave me so much more strength in certain environments. For me, those environments have been backpacker hostels, shared houses, restaurants, bars, nightclubs, and multi-day music festivals, pretty much all places you would have never found me before I started travelling. My cane provides me with a huge sense of security. It makes embarrassing mistakes okay to make. It sparks my self advocacy. Most people have never seen or met someone like me with a cane before. I never saw myself becoming this person who is raising awareness and education on people who are DeafBlind, but that's exactly who I've become and I absolutely love it!

I've advocated myself to the point where people who have gotten to know me really well have actually started advocating on my behalf.

"Hey what does your stick mean?"

"This is a partially blind person's identification cane,

people who are partially blind use it to identify themselves as someone who can't see very well."

"Sooo...you're blind? But you don't look blind."

"But I am, well not completely. I have this cane to indicate that I am a visually impaired person, otherwise people have no idea and just assume that I'm drunk and high."

"Ya. You look so normal."

"Ha. Ya. That's what makes this disability so interesting, the fact that it's invisible."

"So you can see me right now?"

"Ya I can see you, but only when I look directly at you. Your face is completely gone as soon as I look past the side of your head."

"Really?! Hmm. Wow."

"Ya I'm about 70% blind. My vision is like looking through a tunnel, I only see what my central vision scans over, everything else is either black or blurred."

"Wow that's crazy. I would have never known. Let me buy you a beer!"

I have been so empowered by all the nice things people have said to me upon sharing my story with them that I am inspired to keep growing as an advocate and maybe more some day. Here are some of the more common things people have told me.

"You're an inspiration!"

"Meeting you has changed my perspective on life."

"You're a legend!"

"You should write a book or become a motivational speaker."

"I'm so happy to have met you, keep doing what you're doing and living life to the full."

"You give the best hugs!"

I have lived in houses full of people from all over the world who I became really good friends with. I have hitchhiked quite extensively, discovering the true kindness and hospitable nature of Kiwis. I have gone on road trips with new friends and have even driven in some cases. I have had girlfriends from France, Israel, Brazil, Denmark, Germany, Canada and America. I have been guided and helped around nightclubs and festivals by people who have just met me. I have solo tramped an epic and rugged 91 kilometre, eight day, track through one of New Zealand's stunning national parks. I have had life-altering spiritual awakenings, leading to the discovery and love of myself with the universe. I am telling you these things because if it wasn't for me starting to emerge proud of who I am, these things would have never happened.

I could go on and on about how great it's been to accept who I am and do what I've had to do to live this life but the article is already getting too long, so I'm going to leave you now with the key points of inspiration from my story.

Love yourself before trying to love someone else. You're good for more than one person or one company. Question your happiness. Make a positive change in your life. Be adaptable - get out of your comfort zone. Believe in yourself. Challenge the fear of the unknown. Show people that you're not afraid. Be an advocate. Connect with humans. Explore nature. Discover your spiritual side. Strengthen your resilience. Exude perseverance. Express gratitude for what you have. Don't compare yourself to others. Emerge proud and you'll wonder why you ever waited.

My experience in New Zealand has inspired me to dream of one day creating a world where the living abroad lifestyle is more accessible to people with disabilities.

I also dream of meeting more people like you and me, to travel and have a good party with some day.

Kindness, love, and light everyone xoxo :)

Follow Cody on social media:

Facebook: www.facebook.com/cody.campbell.50951

Resources for #Emerging Proud through Sight Loss

UK RESOURCES

BBC Radio 4 – "In Touch" radio programme

www.bbc.co.uk/programmes/b006qxww
Every Tuesday 8.40pm BST/GMT

Blind In Business

Blind in Business helps people who are blind or have partial sight get into the world of work more easily. Their Training and Employment Services help you to identify your ambitions and achieve your goals. They offer help and support with finding work, the interview process, and obtaining the equipment you need to succeed. They also support employers in hiring and working with people with visual impairments.

www.blindinbusiness.org.uk/

The British Computer Association of the Blind

The BCAB promotes the special needs and interests of the visually impaired who either work in the computing field or have an active interest in computing. BCAB is a lively community of blind and partially sighted people. Their members include people of all skill levels, ages and interests.

www.bcab.org.uk

British Blind Sport

British Blind Sport prides itself on making a visible difference through sport as we know that taking the first step into participating in a sporting or recreational activity can change lives for the better.

www.britishblindsport.org.uk

Guide Dogs for the Blind Association

Supporting visually impaired people across the UK.

Phone: 0118 983 5555

Website: www.guidedogs.org.uk

LOOK

Look charity supports young visually impaired people and their families to thrive. They do this through mentoring, transformational events, youth forums and parent support groups.They can also link to other charities and organisations who can help you access the support you need.

www.look-uk.org

National Blind Children's Society

Supporting visually impaired children, young people and their families across the UK

Phone: 01278 764 764 (Head Office)

Website: www.nbcs.org.uk

Royal National Institute for the Blind (RNIB)

RNIB are a charity and membership body of and for blind people and those with sight problems. They will be there for you, your family and all who help you when you need our support.

Phone: 0303 123 9999

Website: www.rnib.org.uk

Scottish Sensory Centre

Based in Edinburgh, Scotland, they promote and support new developments and effective practices in the education of children and young people with sensory impairments ie visual, hearing or dual (deafblindness) sensory impairment.

www.ssc.education.ed.ac.uk

VICTA

VICTA is a national charity that provides support to children and young adults from 0 to 29 who are blind or partially sighted and their families. VICTA believes that everyone has the right to an independent and fulfilling life. VICTA's support, advice, grants and activities enable young people and their families to build skills, develop confidence and help each other toward a more positive future.

www.victa.org.uk

Visionary

Visionary is a membership organisation for local sight loss charities. Our Vision is for a world in which people living with sight loss can access the services they need at a local level where and when they need them. Our Mission is to develop a strong national network of good quality local sight loss organisations, covering all parts of the UK, to help achieve this.

www.visionary.org.uk

Visualise Training and Consultancy

Visualise is all about inclusion and accessibility for people living with visual impairment (VI). This ensures they provide excellent service for customers and employees with VI while meeting their legal obligations under The Equality Act 2010.

www.visualisetrainingandconsultancy.com

Vocal Eyes

Vocal Eyes believe that blind and partially sighted people should have the best possible opportunities to experience and enjoy art and heritage. Their mission is to increase those opportunities, make them as good as possible, and ensure that as many blind and partially sighted people as possible are aware of them, and that the arts and heritage sector know how to create them, and welcome blind and partially sighted people as a core audience.

www.vocaleyes.co.uk

INTERNATIONAL RESOURCES

Alliance for Equality of Blind Canadians

Alliance for Equality of Blind Canadians (AEBC) is a national grassroots, peer support organization that comprises Canadians who are blind, deaf-blind or partially sighted and our supporters from the public at large. We work to ensure we have a voice on all matters affecting our participation in Canada's mainstream society.

www.blindcanadians.ca/

Blind Low Vision NZ

New Zealand's main provider of practical and emotional support for the 11,700 Kiwis who are blind or have low vision, enabling them to face their future with confidence.

www.blindlowvision.org.nz/

The Canadian National Institute for the Blind (CNIB)

Since founding in 1918, CNIB has grown to become the primary resource for Canadians who are blind or partially sighted, with offices in communities across the country.

www.cnib.ca

CAVI

A Cisco Networking Academy based in Perth, Western Australia providing education and career/self development, both nationally and internationally, to people who are totally or partially blind.

www.wiki.cucat.org

Deafblind International (DbI)

Founded over 30 years ago and is the world association promoting services for deafblind people. DbI brings together professionals, researchers, families, deafblind people and administrators to raise awareness of deafblindness. Central to their work is to support the development of services to enable a good quality of life for deafblind children and adults of all ages.

www.deafblindinternational.org

Euro Blind (EBU)

EBU aims to protect and promote the interests of all blind and partially-sighted people in Europe. Its objects and powers are set out in Article II of its Constitution.

www.euroblind.org

Fighting Blindness (Ireland)

An Irish, patient-led charity with a vision to cure blindness, support those experiencing sight loss and empower patients.

www.fightingblindness.ie/

Guide Dog Association of New South Wales (Australia)

Providing information on vision impairments, cane or canine, teacher resources and support services.

www.guidedogs.com.au

Helen Keller International

Founded in 1915, Helen Keller International is dedicated to saving and improving the sight and lives of the world's vulnerable by combatting the causes and consequences of blindness, poor health and malnutrition.

www.hki.org/

Instituto Nacional Para Ciegos (National Institute for the Blind)

The International Agency for the Prevention of Blindness (IAPB) is an alliance of civil society organisations, corporates and professional bodies promoting eye health through advocacy, knowledge and partnerships based in Bogota in Columbia.

www.inci.gov.co

International Blind Sports Federation (IBSA)

Since 1989 when the IPC was founded, IBSA has played a key role in the development of sports for athletes with a visual impairment. The IPC's aspiration is to make for a more inclusive society for people with an impairment through Para sport.

www.ibsasport.org

International Council for Education of People with Visual Impairment (ICEVI)

A global association of individuals and organizations that promotes equal access to appropriate education for all children and youth with visual impairment so that they may achieve their full potential.

www.icevi.org/

Johannesburg Society for the Blind

Working in partnership with disabled people to promote self-help education work skills and independent living skills for Blind and Partially Sighted People.

www.icon.co.za/~jhbblindsoc

The Lighthouse International

A leading resource worldwide on vision impairment and vision rehabilitation, based in New York USA.

www.lighthouseguild.org

National Education Centre for Blind Children: ChildVision

Based in Ireland and dedicated to the education and therapy needs of blind and multi-disabled children.

www.childvision.ie

Shree Ramana Maharishi Academy for the Blind (SRMAB)

SRMAB was founded in 1969 in India with the motto "Service to Humanity is service to God" by Sri. T V Srinivasan, Late Sri. Thirumurthy and friends.

www.srmab.org.in/

South African National Council for the Blind

The Council's Vision is to facilitate a network of organisations who collaborate towards the prevention of blindness and securing the full participation and inclusion of blind and partially sighted people in all aspects of a diverse South African society.

www.sancb.org.za

South Australian Royal Society for the Blind (Australia)

The RSB is the primary source of assistance giving people with a vision impairment the opportunity to improve the quality and independence of their lives

www.rsb.org.au

De Vereniging Bartiméus

Based in The Netherlands, this is the leading institute for visually impaired people and support services.

www.bartimeus.nl

Vision Australia

Assisting people who are blind and vision impaired to maximize their opportunities by providing specialist staff, information and technology resources that meet individual needs.

www.visionaustralia.org/

VisionServe Alliance

VisionServe Alliance is a consortium of Executive Directors/CEOs of 501 nonprofits throughout the United States that provide unique and specialized services to people who are blind or with severe vision loss. We bring together the full diversity of services for one conversation with the ultimate goal of unifying the many issues and organizations operating independently of one another in the field.

www.visionservealliance.org/

World Blind Union (WBU)

The World Blind Union (WBU) is the internationally recognized organization, representing the 285 million blind and partially sighted persons in 190 member countries. They speak to governments and international bodies on issues concerning blindness and visual impairments in conjunction with their members. WBU brings together all the major national and international organizations of blind persons and those organizations providing services to the visually impaired to work on the issues affecting the quality of life for blind people.

www.worldblindunion.org

*The resources in the above lists are taken from those indicated as helpful by the #Emerging Proud community when consulted specifically for this project. They are examples, and by no means meant as an exclusive list.

Vision

"Vision is not limited to physically 'seeing'. Vision is not limited to the information passed from our eyes to our brain. There's another type of vision. It is the ability to look at ourselves and see what we CAN do, not what we cannot do.

Truth is, I CAN still laugh, smile, listen, talk, teach, dance, hug, love, and be happy. Vision loss can hold you down, but the truth will set you free."

— Maria Johnson, *Girl Gone Blind.*

Acknowledgements

My infinite thanks go to the incredible team behind the #Emerging Proud book series; the book Reps, and especially Yvette Chivers for spearheading this particular edition in the series, our Publishing Guru, Sean Patrick, of *That Guy's House*, and Editor extraordinaire Mandy Horne, all of whom have passionately, and without question, donated their time and expertise in order to support this book series to fruition. It's a vision we all share, and one that would not have been possible to achieve without each and every one of us coming together, with no agenda other than wanting to disseminate hope like confetti around the world…

The team also extends our immense gratitude to everyone in this pocket book; those who have bravely gifted their personal transformation story with the hope that it helps at least one other person in the world to find their own inner spark to initiate or aid their recovery journey. We aim for these books to create a 'positive domino effect', rippling out HOPE to those who need it most.

Our gratitude also goes to The Missing Kind charity (www.missingkind.org) who seed-funded this book series as an official Sponsor. The Missing Kind also helped to fund the Eye Inspire project with a start up grant.

Without all of these team players there would be no HOPE confetti, so together we celebrate the incredible power of heart-founded collaboration, and a shared vision and mission.

Other titles in our Kinda Proud Pocket Books of Hope and Transformation series so far:

#Emerging Proud through NOTEs (non-ordinary transcendent experiences)

#Emerging Proud through Disordered Eating, Body Image and Low Self-Esteem

#Emerging Proud through Suicide

#Emerging Proud through Trauma and Abuse

And due for publication soon;

Muslims #Emerging Proud through Mental Distress

Offical Sponsors

Sync Inspire CIC (Community Interest Company) is a not-for-profit organisation giving back through various projects to help support people and the environment.

The main areas of our business are:

- venue management and event planning
- streaming events and conferences online
- social media management and marketing
- carpentry and building work
- bespoke wood designs (including upcycling)

We also run two creative and performance projects:

- B-Side Project
  (music development and education)
- Circus Dionysus
  (event performance and workshops)

Our current outreach and invested profits are focused on the Eye Inspire project

For more information please visit;
www.syncinspire.org and www.eyeinspire.org

VISUALISE
Training and Consultancy

Visualise Training and Consultancy is all about inclusion and accessibility for people living with visual impairment (VI). Visualise Founder Daniel Williams has Retinitis Pigmentosa, so he established the business in 2014 to share his experience and expertise with businesses and organisations - ensuring that businesses provide excellent services for customers and employees with VI whilst meeting their legal obligations under The Equality Act 2010.

www.visualisetrainingandconsultancy.co.uk

"Blindness is not an excuse to make me worthless and weak. It made me realize my worth and capability, it allowed me to become stronger, capable and more independent."

— The Invisible Vision Project

"Only in the darkness can you see the stars"

— Martin Luther King

Lightning Source UK Ltd.
Milton Keynes UK
UKHW020710030222
398149UK00009B/334